HISTORIC ROYAL PALACES

THE
CORONATION
CEREMONY

OF THE
KINGS AND QUEENS OF ENGLAND
AND
THE CROWN JEWELS

TESSA ROSE

London: HMSO

ISBN 0 11 701361 7
Printed in the UK for HMSO
Dd. 294658 C15 5/92

Written by Tessa Rose
Designed by HMSO Graphic Design: Guy Myles Warren
Picture Research by Gill Metcalfe.

HMSO publications are available from:

HMSO Publications Centre
(Mail, fax and telephone orders only)
PO Box 276, London, SW8 5DT
Telephone orders 071-873 9090
General enquiries 071-873 0011
(queuing system in operation for both numbers)
Fax orders 071-873 8200

HMSO Bookshops
49 High Holborn, London, WC1V 6HB
(counter service only)
071-873 0011   Fax 071-873 8200
258 Broad Street, Birmingham, B1 2HE
021-643 3740   Fax 021-643 6510
Southey House, 33 Wine Street, Bristol, BS1 2BQ
0272 264306   Fax 0272 294515
9–21 Princess Street, Manchester, M60 8AS
061-834 7201   Fax 061-833 0634
16 Arthur Street, Belfast, BT1 4GD
0232 238451   Fax 0232 235401
71 Lothian Road, Edinburgh, EH3 9AZ
031-228 4181   Fax 031-229 2734

HMSO's Accredited Agents
(see Yellow Pages)

and through good booksellers

Contents

The vast majority of the two million or so people of all nationalities who file through the Jewel House in the Tower of London each year undoubtedly do so because the Tower – with Buckingham Palace, the Houses of Parliament and Westminster Abbey – is one of the capital's compulsory tourist sights. A high proportion no doubt also visit the Jewel House because of both the world-wide reputation of the remarkable collection of precious objects, and especially of precious stones, it contains, and the glamour of the association between them and the British monarchy. The number of those who are interested in the Regalia – popularly known as the Crown Jewels – as such, and the objects associated with them, or have any knowledge of their specific use, or understanding of their great historical, and former profoundly religious, significance is probably very small indeed, and is likely always to remain so. There must, however, be many visitors who would like to know more about them and their history than is given in the popular guide-books, but have been unable to do so because no work in which they could find further information of this kind has been in print for many years. The present book answers the long-felt need for such a work by combining a fully-illustrated account of the objects, their history and function, with an up-to-date survey of the coronation ceremonies and their development since early-medieval times, written with the non-specialist in mind.

The book is based partly on a major catalogue *raisonné*, although the choice of illustrations and the captions are the author's own. The catalogue is the first ever produced of the contents of the Jewel House, and has been written, under my editorship, by a group of seven distinguished scholars, whose original researches have brought to light a great deal of new information, not only about the objects now displayed at the Tower, but also about their predecessors – mostly destroyed after the execution of Charles I in 1649 – and about the history of the coronation itself. The scholars in question are Mrs Shirley Bury, Mr A.G. Grimwade, Dr R. Harding, Mr E.A. Jobbins, Mr D.B. King, Mr R.W. Lightbown, and Mr K. Scarrat, and grateful thanks are due to all of them for agreeing to allow Tessa Rose to consult and use their unpublished material for her own book.

CLAUDE BLAIR

Foreword

THE WORD CORONATION immediately conjures up an image of a crown being placed on a monarch's head in formal acknowledgement of his or her right to rule. The Roman method of inaugurating an emperor had reflected the fact that he was chosen for the office: election by the Senate was followed by acclamation by army and people. Even after the elective principle had become sullied by army coups and the dynastic ambitions of the emperors themselves, the form of the ceremony remained unchanged. Roman emperors copied the Eastern practice of wearing a diadem, a wreath-like crown, but there is no evidence to suggest that it was received in a prescribed ritual.

Election was also the principle for succession among the early warrior kings, including those of England. In general, an important attribute of kingship was descent from the gods. All members of the ruling royal

The Making of Kings

The English coronation ritual has its roots in both the pagan and Christian worlds. Election, the principle of succession among the early English warrior kings, was borrowed from the Romans. By his imposition of a dictatorship through military conquest, Julius Caesar, depicted here in the final canvas of the fifteenth century artist Andrea Mantegna's 'The Triumphs of Caesar', reduced the principles of election by the Senate and the consent of the people to mere forms. They would remain, however, potent influences in the subsequent development of the coronation rite.

family could claim this distinction, and it was from among their number that the new leader was normally chosen. The election was decided by members of the kingly family and the nobles or elders of the tribe. Military prowess was highly valued in those violent and unstable times and the most likely reason for a successful claim. What is known of early inaugural ceremonies suggests that they were primarily public acclamations of the new ruler and his might as a warrior. It was common practice among the Germanic tribes for the king to receive the acclamation while standing on an infantry shield held aloft by warriors; the Germans used to shake the shield. In time the king was placed on a throne instead of a shield.

Election and elevation would remain indispensable inaugural rites in western Europe until well into the fourteenth century and they still form part of the English coronation ceremony. However, they would be gradually eclipsed by the twin, and originally separate, rites of consecration by unction and crowning. When these rites became conjoined in one ceremony, the inauguration of kings assumed the familiar form that we know today and call coronation.

Consecration by unction is essentially an ecclesiastical ritual by which a person is made sacred by anointing him with holy oil and chrism. Its use in relation to kings came about as a result of the spread of Christianity and, in particular, a new ideology devised by the Church in Rome. The collapse of the western part of the Roman empire, in 476 AD, had allowed the papacy to nourish ambitions of claiming for itself, in the absence of imperial rule, the spiritual leadership of all peoples outside the territory of the eastern part of the empire. This leadership was disputed by the emperor in Byzantium, who described himself as Vice-Regent of Christ and, despite lacking the power to shape events in the West, maintained his supremacy over the papacy in Rome. The popes in Rome, meanwhile, called themselves Vicars of Christ and claimed a special authority over kings. Papal justification for this claim was based on the belief that it was the popes who would have to answer for secular rulers on the Day of Judgement. The Bible gives many examples of God sanctioning the appointment of kings, and of holy men being used as His

THE CORONATION CEREMONY AND THE CROWN JEWELS

3

instrument for inaugurating them. The Church used such biblical models to support their claim. In the first book of Kings the prophet Samuel is directed by God to anoint Saul, the man chosen to save the Israelites from the Philistines. When Saul later proves unsatisfactory, God chooses David to replace him as king. Both Saul and David are marked out from the rest of humankind and made sacred as God's chosen ones by the act of anointing them with oil. Unction was believed to confer God's grace and goodness on a ruler so that he might perform his kingly duties better and to cause him to be held in greater honour by his people.

On a more mundane level, kings used unction as a means of legitimizing their own right to rule and securing the succession for their sons. The first recorded instance of royal unction in England occurred in 787, when Offa of Mercia had his son Ecgfrith anointed. Offa was overlord of all the kings in England, a position he had won and secured through feat of arms. The anointing of Ecgfrith may be read as an attempt to protect the royal line against usurpers. In the event, Ecgfrith survived his father by a mere six months before being deposed by Cenwulf, Offa's fourth cousin twice removed.

Offa's decision to use unction was probably influenced by the example of the newly established Carolingian kings of the Franks in western Europe. The first of these, Pippin, had dethroned the powerless but long-established and sacred Merovingian dynasty – famed for their traditional royal symbol of long hair – and had himself anointed by the leading churchman of the Franks, St Boniface. Three years later, in 754, Pippin had himself anointed again, this time by Pope Stephen II, an act which put his succession, and that of his sons after him, beyond dispute. Pippin's sons Charles (later to become Charles the Great or Charlemagne) and Carloman were blessed at the same ceremony and confirmed as Pippin's heirs. The Pope threatened with interdict and excommunication any who dared to 'elect a king born from another's womb and not from the union of those [Pippin and his wife Bertha] whom the Divine mercy has deigned to exalt and to confirm and consecrate'. Charlemagne would be anointed again on his succession, in 768, and in 781 would have his two little sons, Pippin and Louis, anointed as kings by the Pope. (Second unction was declared unlawful by the papacy in the late ninth century, bringing to an end a practice – unnecessary in Rome's eyes – which kings viewed as a way of renewing God's grace.) The association between Church and king established by these inaugurations would last until 1914.

Unction gained so much favour with kings in Germany, France and England that by the tenth and eleventh centuries it was the norm rather than the exception. Kings elsewhere could rule without unction – there are many examples in western Europe, even as late as the twelfth and thirteenth centuries. However, the higher status accorded to kings that had been both crowned and anointed was sought after. The kings of Scotland, for example, were eager to gain the privilege of unction to add fuel to their claim of independence from England. They were petitioning hard in the mid-thirteenth century and were not granted it until 1329.

Charlemagne was the first king to incorporate the formula 'King by the grace of God' (Dei gratia rex) into his title. The Carolingians were the most powerful and the most Christian of Western kings, and the papacy came increasingly to rely on them. Charlemagne believed, as did his forebears, that he possessed the power to create kings without the mediation of the Church. In 813 he personally crowned his son Louis. The idea that kingship derived from anointing by a churchman or required the Church's confirmation would not be widely accepted for several centuries more.

Medieval kings always regarded the rite as a deeply serious matter and one not to be undertaken lightly. The Church's conception of kingship imposed certain obligations on Christian rulers. It was a ruler's responsibility, for example, to help and protect the Church and also to join with it in the task of maintaining a Christian society. The Church expected him to fulfil the secular and spiritual role, after the biblical model of Melchizedek, who is described as king and priest in the book of Genesis. King Edgar put off his anointing until 973, 14 years after his crowning, because only then did he feel ready to maintain the standards of self-restraint and self-discipline that unction required of him. Failure to do so might invite God's wrath.

The Church did not claim a central role in the crowning of emperors until AD 800, when the papacy stepped in, quite literally, and

In medieval England, kings and their court clerics entertained a semi-priestly conception of the office of an anointed king. This is evident in the deliberate attempt to style the king's coronation and death robes after priestly vestments. Henry VI, depicted here with St Edmund, the martyr king killed in 870 by the Danes for refusing to renounce Christianity, is said to have worn 'byshop's gere' at his coronation in 1429. Orthodox clerical doctine, however, denied to kings any jurisdiction in spiritual matters.

solemnized the ritual. The occasion was Charlemagne's coronation as emperor in St Peter's Basilica on Christmas Day. Pope Leo III placed a crown on the Frankish King's head, much to the displeasure of Charlemagne who, according to the contemporary chronicler Einhard, declared that he would never have entered the church if he had known of the Pope's intention beforehand. Leo's boldness resulted in the Church establishing the sole right to crown future emperors of what would much later become known as the Holy Roman Empire.

The Pope's decision to crown Charlemagne emperor, effectively reviving the imperial title that had lain vacant since the overthrow of Romolus Augustolus by the Ostrogoth Odoacer in 476, was influenced by events in the East. In AD 800 the Byzantine ruler was not only a woman, the Empress Irene, but a usurper and evil-doer who had seized power after murdering her son, Constantine VI. Charlemagne's immense power and his commitment to Christianity and its aims recommended him to the papacy in preference to Irene. On a personal level, Leo had every reason for wanting to show his gratitude to Charlemagne. Shortly before the historic crowning in St Peter's, Charlemagne had acquitted Leo of charges of adultery and perjury. The coronation was clearly intended to strengthen the bond between the papacy and Charlemagne. Almost certainly, however, Leo did not foresee that a new dynasty of emperors would result from his action.

Charlemagne was almost certainly not anointed as well as crowned on his assumption of the imperial title. The first occasion on which unction and crowning were indisputably combined in one ceremony was the imperial coronation of Louis I, Charlemagne's son, at Rheims in 816. Pope Stephen brought with him from Rome a crown of gold and precious stones, setting a precedent that would last well into the twelfth century.

According to the popes, this crown had formerly belonged to Constantine, the first Roman emperor to be baptized. The notion came into being that an emperor could only be crowned by a pope. Further, the idea of overlordship, or suzerainty, came to attach itself to the gift of a crown. Eventually, in 1338, the Holy Roman Empire would formally reassert the principle that election alone created an emperor.

The revival of the imperial title did not establish Charlemagne and his successors as overlords of the rulers of the other western kingdoms, and despite claims to the contrary, in reality the territories of the Holy Roman Empire were restricted to France (until the fall of the Carolingian dynasty), Germany and Italy. In the main, English kings stoutly declared and maintained their independence. When Louis of Bavaria, the new Holy Roman Emperor, commanded Edward III to kiss his feet the English King refused on the grounds that, as an anointed ruler, he was free of subjection to the empire. English kings regarded themselves as imperial because they claimed to have no earthly overlord and because of the prestige attaching to those who ruled over more than one kingdom. Athelstan, for example, used the title 'imperator' after conquering the kingdom of Northumbria, in 927, and becoming ruler of all the kingdoms of England.

The papacy did, though, believe that it could create kings in lands not ruled by the Holy Roman Emperor. The popes would send crowns to their appointees, following a practice borrowed from Byzantium. In 1173, for example, Henry II received from Pope Lucius a crown of gold and peacock feathers together with an order granting Ireland to his son John. The practice of bestowing crowns was followed by that of bestowing sceptres, and these two items became the most potent symbols of kingly power.

The interest taken in the symbolism of royal office by the ninth-century Frankish King Charles the Bald led to the development of coronation, in the sense of crowning and unction, as a liturgical ritual that was to be performed with every new accession. In England the ritual became fairly well established in the tenth century as the way of marking the accession

The potential for conflict between the Church of Rome and the monarchy was realized with a vengeance in the reign of Henry VIII. Henry's break with Rome made the Church of England as independent of the papacy as the Crown of England was independent of the Holy Roman Emperor. Henry is depicted here arriving for his meeting with the French king Francis I at the Field of Cloth of Gold, near Calais, an event which took place in 1520.

of a new king. Ecclesiastical coronation legitimized and honoured the king who was crowned, and established a lawful dynasty with a fixed right of succession to the throne. The importance that men, especially kings, came to attach to the symbolic act of coronation is perhaps well illustrated by the following. In 1037, Harold, the illegitimate son of King Canute and murderer of another royal claimant, Alfred the

THE CORONATION CEREMONY AND THE CROWN JEWELS

Aetheling, asked Archbishop Aethelnoth of Canterbury to consecrate him and to give him the crown and sceptre which Canute had passed to Aethelnoth for safekeeping. Harold was already the king in the sense that he had been elected to the office and received formal recognition by a council of nobles. And yet it would seem that, in his own eyes at least, this was no longer enough to legitimize a claim to the throne.

THE CORONATION CEREMONY AND THE CROWN JEWELS

The early medieval period, and indeed later centuries, was dogged by an on-going battle of ideologies between emperors and kings on the one hand and the Church on the other. Kings did not accept the Church's notion that as the recipients of unction they were in effect inferior to the men who bestowed it, nor that imperial and kingly power could not exist independently of clerical sanction. Acceptance of the Church's viewpoint would have acknowledged the primacy of their authority over that of kings. The kings of France and England gradually altered their view of kingship, replacing the idea of divine ordinance through unction forming the basis of their right to rule with that of divine ordinance by the succession of a rightful heir of royal blood.

In medieval England many people regarded the king's office as a 'mixed' state, both lay and clerical, with some jurisdiction in spiritual matters. The first English ruler to exercise this jurisdiction was Henry VIII, although he did so for reasons of necessity rather than conviction. Had it not been for the fact that his queen Catherine of Aragon was the aunt of the most powerful sovereign in Europe, Charles V, and that the Pope, Clement VII, dared not offend him, it is likely that Henry would have reached an accommodation with the Church of Rome over his request for a divorce. As it was, however, after several futile attempts to settle the problem and with Anne Boleyn now pregnant, possibly with the male heir he so desperately wanted, Henry decided to force the issue. To obtain a divorce he resorted to an authority at his command, Parliament.

The Act of Restraint of Appeals and the Act of Supremacy set the seal to one of the most important changes in England's history. Henry's proclamation that he was the sole earthly power in his empire and his adoption of the title 'Supreme Head of the Church of England' signalled the end of papal authority in England. It signalled, too, the end of religious harmony and created dangerous tensions that would surface in the reign of the Stuarts.

Although the establishment of the hereditary principle of succession, or primogeniture, in the mid-thirteenth century reduced the real signifi-

During his 25-year reign, Charles II is estimated to have touched something like 100,000 sufferers of the skin disease scrofula, which a sovereign's touch was said to cure. Part of the ritual involved making the sign of the cross over each sufferer while holding a gold coin in his hand. The coin would subsequently be hung round the patient's neck. After 1665 the real coin was replaced by a specially struck medal which had no value as currency.

cance of unction, the rite would continue for several more centuries to exert a powerful hold over men's imaginations. Laypeople, clergy and royalty shared the belief that anointment conferred sacredness. Elizabeth I would delay in ordering the execution of Mary, Queen of Scots, partly because she was reluctant to send an anointed ruler to the scaffold. Much of the lengthy argument concerning the trial and execution of Charles I centred on the sanctity of the king and his divine right to rule as he saw fit. Charles would maintain to the last that 'a subject and a sovereign are clean different things'.

The miraculous powers attributed to kings as a manifestation of divine approval were widely believed in until at least the eighteenth century.

The Royal Gift of Healing.

The rite of touching for scrofula — an unsightly though not fatal disease of the glands in the neck — is the best documented example. The practice was introduced into England from France in about the early twelfth century. A genuinely royal hand was needed to effect a cure for the disease, known as the 'king's evil' in England. Groups of sufferers would be brought before the monarch, who would touch each person in turn and then make the sign of the cross over their sores. Among the thousands brought before Queen Anne, the last English monarch to perform the rite, was the 30-month-old Samuel Johnson. The royal touch would, his mother hoped, cure his bad eyes.

James I was not alone among Protestants in seeing only superstition in the ritual. The political upheavals that engulfed his successors, Charles I and James II, would result in a general shattering of faith in the mystique of royalty. The otherness formerly conferred on monarchs would, however, continue to be reflected in the ritual of coronation.

THE ESTABLISHMENT OF A REGALIA specifically or largely for use at English coronations has taken many centuries. In the early medieval period the term regalia was taken to mean a collection of robes and ornaments worn by the king on all great ceremonial occasions and whenever he wished to appear in his royal state. Each king had for his coronation and also for state ceremonies a personal regalia, and this might include hereditary items as well as ones specially made for him. The most important ceremonial occasions for the use of the personal regalia in early times were the solemn festivals of Christmas, Easter and Whitsun. In the late Middle Ages the king would also appear in his royal state on Twelfth Night or at the opening of Parliament. A separate set of personal ornaments and robes used exclusively for the coronation ritual was not established until the reign of Edward III. The great crown was the only item worn on other occasions besides coronation.

The prime movers in the establishment of a hereditary coronation regalia were probably the Abbots of Westminster. In the 1130s the Prior of Westminster, Osbert of Clare, produced forged documents to support the Abbey's claim to be the rightful place of coronation of all English kings. They maintained that Edward the Confessor (died 1066) had left his own regalia in the Abbey's care so that it should be used in the coronation of future kings. It seems that, in some way, Edward the Confessor either constituted a hereditary coronation regalia or that Westminster Abbey persuaded themselves and the Normans that a regalia he had left in their custody was intended for future coronations. In either case, St Edward's regalia – the Confessor was canonized in 1161 – is the first well-authenticated instance in European history of the constitution of a hereditary coronation regalia.

Among the most important items in St Edward's regalia were a crown, sceptre, rod, a large chalice and paten, a cross and rich robes. Little

The Origins of the Regalia

Bronze effigy of Edward III, Westminster Abbey. The practice of keeping the coronation vestments and regalia separate from the royal ornaments and robes worn on other occasions, such as at the solemn festivals of Christmas, Easter and Whitsun, was first documented in 1356 during the reign of Edward III.

is known of the part played by this regalia in twelfth-century coronations, although the presumption is that it was used to crown each king in succession. From the time when Henry III is expressly said to have been crowned with St Edward's Crown — at his second coronation in 1220 — the greatest importance was attached to the Confessor's regalia.

The authority of the kings of England was strengthened by the inheritance of a crown associated with a monarch officially recognized as a saint. Henry III encouraged the cult of the saint. He had a fresco depicting the coronation of the Confessor set above the head of his bed in his great chamber, known as the Painted Chamber, in the Palace of Westminster. In the fourteenth century it was believed that St Edward's Crown had originally belonged to King Alfred. This enhanced the crown's significance: antiquity could now be added to its mystique as a holy relic.

Richard II shared his forebear's exceptionally keen interest in the coronation and its antiquities. He liked to show the regalia to visiting foreign dignitaries. Among these was the King of Armenia, Louis de Lusignan, whom Richard took to the Abbey one January evening in 1386 for a

THE CORONATION CEREMONY AND THE CROWN JEWELS

THE CORONATION CEREMONY AND THE CROWN JEWELS

15

Bronze effigy of Richard II, Westminster Abbey. English kings regarded St Edward's regalia as royal property and the Abbot and monks of Westminster merely as its custodians. Richard II, for example, who took a great interest in St Edward's regalia and its history, delighted in showing it to visiting dignitaries. One such visitor, Louis de Lusignan, he took personally to the Abbey after dark and showed him the regalia by candlelight. The treasure kept in the Tower of London (opposite) *was similarly a source of pride to medieval kings.*

viewing by candlelight of the splendours of the royal regalia. Some thirteen years later Richard would mark his own abdication in favour of Henry Bolingbroke (Henry IV) with the symbolic gesture of surrendering the crown, and thus his kingly power, to his rival.

Although royal property, St Edward's regalia remained under the perpetual custody of Westminster Abbey until the Civil War. It may be that Edward, in depositing the regalia in the Abbey, was originally motivated by ideas of security. Kings after Edward the Confessor tackled the problem of keeping the treasure safe by parcelling it out to various monasteries, theft from which would be sacrilege. King John, for example, deposited treasure in monasteries as far apart as Furness and Fountains in the north to Amesbury and Croydon in the south. So widely did he disperse the treasure about his kingdom that Henry III, his son, had to send to the royal castle of Corfe for the regalia for his second coronation in 1220.

Under Henry the Tower of London became the main royal treasury and the repository of regalia other than St Edward's, which remained under the care of the Abbots of Westminster. Edward I, Henry's son, decided

to transfer from the Tower much of the treasure and deposit it in a new treasury built under the crypt of the new Westminster chapter-house. Edward's decision was sensible given that the Palace of Westminster was the principal royal residence in London at that time and also the centre of the royal administration. However, the new treasury did not prove as secure as the Tower and in 1303 its contents were burgled. The treasure was eventually recovered and then promptly sent back to the Tower for safe-keeping.

St Edward's regalia remained in the Westminster treasury and was periodically added to. The monarch's orb and the bracelets, for example, were eventually handed over by the Tower to be kept with the Westminster regalia some time between 1606 and 1649.

The history of the medieval regalia ends abruptly in 1649 with the triumph of the Parliamentary army over Charles I. The Commonwealth authorities regarded the regalia as 'monuments of superstition and idolatry' and seem to have been intent on their destruction. By the end of January 1650 virtually all of St Edward's regalia and the crowns and ensigns of Tudor and Stuart monarchy had been broken up, the metal melted down and jewels sold. The sole exception was the anointing spoon.

The Commonwealth quickly crumbled after the death of Oliver Cromwell, opening the way for the restoration of the monarchy in the person of Charles II. A new regalia was required to replace the items lost during

The Tower treasury seems to have become the main royal treasury under Henry III, who was a keen collector of jewels. Additional rooms were set aside to accommodate the burgeoning treasure until in the sixteenth century a new jewel house was built adjoining the south front of the Tower. This long, low two-storeyed building with a tower at its western end was destroyed under the Commonwealth. This illustration shows the Tower complex as it was in the reign of Henry VIII, after the expansion.

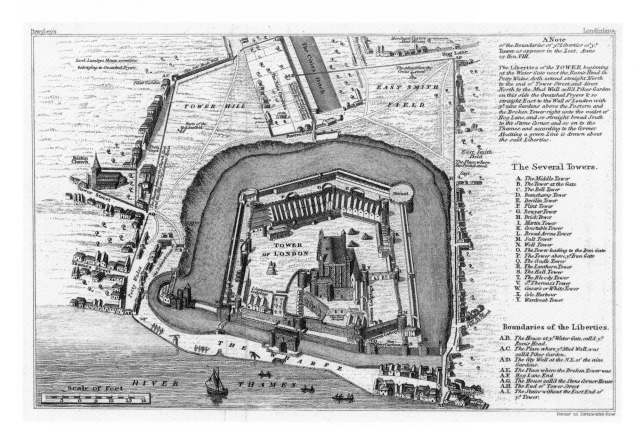

THE CORONATION CEREMONY AND THE CROWN JEWELS

Charles II returned to England from exile in the Dutch town of Breda on 26 May 1660. Among the large party of followers to land with him at Dover on that day was Sir Edward Walker, who would play a crucial role in the preparations for Charles's coronation. It would fall to Walker to produce a memorandum on the procedure to be followed for the coronation together with a list of the ornaments required to replace the ornaments lost in the Cromwell era.

'the late unhappy times', the words of Sir Edward Walker, Garter Principal King of Arms and Clerk of the Privy Council, who had the task of drawing up a list of all the desiderata, including the regalia, for Charles II's coronation. Only one set of regalia was proposed to replace the two sets used in coronations before the Civil War.

The banker and businessman Robert (later Sir Robert) Viner was commissioned to provide the new royal ornaments. No craftsman himself, Viner distributed the work to others, paying them out of his own pocket in the expectation that the Treasury would settle the total, including his percentage as middle man, of £31,978.9s.11d. Half the bill remained unpaid when he was commissioned to supply further jewels

THE CORONATION CEREMONY AND THE CROWN JEWELS

and plate to Charles. At the Restoration the King had relinquished his feudal rights in exchange for an income based on excise duties granted by Parliament. This income was expected to cover expenses incurred for the conduct of affairs of state as well as his own personal expenditure. However, the King's actual expenditure far exceeded his income. Viner was among those to suffer from the shortfall. In 1683/4 he was bankrupted.

Treasury officials constantly exercised with the problem of making ends meet hit on one major cost-cutting policy after the coronation of Charles II. In future the major jewels embellishing all but the State Crown would be hired. This practice continued up to and including the coronation of George IV in 1821, falling off sharply thereafter and ceasing altogether in 1902.

All the items made for the new regalia were put in the care of the Master of the Jewel House at the Tower. The Jewel House has been open to paying visitors since the 1660s, when individuals could gain access by

The Crown Jewels on display in Wakefield Tower, c.1875. The Tower became a permanent showplace for the regalia in the nineteenth century. The keepership of the Jewel House became a highly prized office in the sixteenth and seventeenth centuries, mainly because of the lucrative perks that went with the position. The Keeper was provided with accommodation and victuals and, from 1547, a role in the coronation itself. He was allowed to walk in the opening procession and to deliver the bracelets. At the banquet afterwards he was seated with the barons.

THE CORONATION CEREMONY AND THE CROWN JEWELS

The regalia has not been safe from attack or burglary even in the Tower. Perhaps the most famous attempt to steal the Crown Jewels was that made by Captain Thomas Blood and his accomplices in 1671. After he was caught Blood refused to speak to anyone but Charles II and was taken to Whitehall for an audience. The Irishman is said to have so charmed the King that he was not only pardoned – as were his accomplices – but also given a pension of £500 per annum and estates in Ireland.

approaching the Keeper or his agent. It became a permanent public showplace in the nineteenth century.

However, the regalia has not been completely safe from attack even in the Tower. A daring attempt to steal the Crown Jewels was made in 1671, causing damage to the orb, or globe, as well as to Charles II's imperial state crown. The leader of the thieves, Captain Thomas Blood, took a mallet to the arches of the crown so that he could conceal it more easily beneath his cloak. After a brief period of imprisonment in the Tower, Blood and his fellow conspirators were pardoned by Charles, much to most people's surprise. A 'bold impudent fellow', according to the diarist John Evelyn, Blood was perhaps a government spy.

Blood & his Accomplices *making their* Efcape *after* Stealing *the* Crown *from the* TOWER *of* LONDON.

Lodge Sculp.

THE CORONATION CEREMONY AND THE CROWN JEWELS

THE REGALIA DELIVERED TO SOVEREIGNS and, when appropriate, queen-consorts during coronation are part of a special set of ornaments now preserved from reign to reign for use in the ceremony. These items – crowns, sceptres, sword, spurs, bracelets and rings – reveal much about the history and meaning of the coronation ceremony, through their design, the materials of which they are made and, in some cases, their origin. They are what is generally understood as the regalia proper. Also classified as regalia but not discussed here are the royal robes, maces and secular and altar plate in the Tower, all of which have been used in coronation ceremonies.

Four items which now form part of the royal regalia pre-date the Restoration: the anointing spoon, the sword known as Curtana and the two Swords of Justice, which are early seventeenth century. Charles I's Yeoman of the Removing Wardrobe, Clement Kinnersley, had bought the spoon in 1649, preserved it and then handed it back to the Crown

The Symbols of Kingship

The regalia produced for the coronation of Charles II in 1661 were remade after 'the old names, and fashion' of the items lost in 1649. Below are some of the items of the modern regalia: St Edward's Crown; the two sceptres; the Sword of Offering; the bracelets; the ring; and the ampulla and spoon.

A scene from the Bayeux Tapestry showing Edward the Confessor with his successor, Harold, and a friend. Edward is wearing an open crown with high points topped with fleurons. The sceptre in his left hand has the fleur-de-lis shaped head generally found on early European sceptres. Precise details of the crowns worn by English kings in the early medieval period are virtually non-existent. The earliest crown for which scholars have anything like a detailed description is the ornament made for William the Conqueror between his victory at Hastings and his coronation. However, there seems clear evidence – both visual and literary – that Edward was responsible for changing the open crown of his predecessors into a closed crown.

at the Restoration. Kinnersley's loyalty was rewarded by Charles II, who re-appointed him to his old position.

The ornaments traditionally delivered to the monarch during the coronation ceremony as symbols of kingship have varied in minor details. For instance, bracelets or armills have not been consistently used, while the significance of St Edward's Staff was lost before the Restoration and since then has only ever been carried in procession. An understanding of the significance of the principal items is central to an understanding of the ritual of coronation.

The Crowns

The crown is the chief symbol of royal power. The Latin terms used in Anglo-Saxon and Norman to describe different types of crown – stemma, corona and diadema – were all borrowed from the head-ornaments of the ancient world. The Romans regarded the crown as a symbol of victory and their emperors, after crowning, as victors of the world. The stemma and corona – originally wreaths or garlands – were worn by the emperors on their accession and as festal ornaments. In its original form the diadema was a fillet, or piece of cloth, worn round the head and tied at the back. A badge of royalty worn by Persian rulers, the diadema was a despised ensign in Republican Rome because of this association. It came into regular use in Rome only at the end of the empire when the Emperor Diocletian (284–305) took to wearing one. Diocletian's diadema was said to have been set with precious stones between a double row of pearls. Constantine (324–37), the first Roman emperor to be baptised, habitually wore a diadema.

Precise details of crowns worn by English kings before the late medieval and Renaissance periods are very sparse. The earliest detailed description of a crown worn by a king at his coronation dates from the ceremony for William the Conqueror in 1066. Pictorial sources, such as coinage, are not reliable because images were often copied from foreign coins or from stylized models. The coins issued during the reigns of Athelstan and Edgar show the kings wearing a circlet-crown with four high points

THE CORONATION CEREMONY AND THE CROWN JEWELS

surmounted by balls and with pendent strings. Edgar was also depicted wearing a circlet-crown in which the points terminate as bipartite fleurons. Canute and Edward the Confessor are shown on some coins wearing tall, pointed crowns shaped like a helmet and on others wearing crowns with high points topped with fleurons.

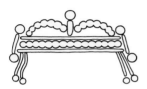

It is certain, however, that the English kings were influenced in their choice of styles by the Byzantine emperors. Edward is thought to have been the first English king to wear the imperial stemma, or closed style of crown, introduced in the sixth century by the Byzantine Emperor Justinian. His predecessors, the evidence suggests, had worn open crowns. It would seem that the stemma was originally a gold circlet usually set with a large precious stone in the centre and surmounted by a round-headed ornament topped by three precious stones over the front.

Edward commissioned a crown of this type from a monk called Spearhavoc, who was also a master-goldsmith, in 1051. The King handed over to Spearhavoc, who had become bishop designate of London thanks to Edward's patronage, gold and fine jewels specially collected for use in the new crown. Edward's desire for an imperial ensign was not to be gratified as quickly as he anticipated, however, because no sooner had Spearhavoc received the precious materials than he promptly absconded with them. The crown, later called St Edward's Crown, was probably made after Edward accumulated yet another collection of gold and stones.

Descriptions of St Edward's Crown suggest that it was a circlet with four fleurons and possibly also four crosses. Between these would have run a double arch. It was possibly decorated with filigree as well as with precious stones and small circular cloisonné enamels, the latter perhaps containing heads of Christ and the saints or holy prophets and kings. The arches and fleurons would also have been set with precious stones and possibly with enamels too. According to the inventory taken by the Commonwealth in 1649, the crown weighed 79½ ounces (troy).

The kings of medieval England required crowns for many occasions, both solemn and festal, and had them specially made or bought for their use.

The headgear worn at less solemn festivities took the form of small crowns, coronals and garlands that were lightweight and low-profiled. The crowns intended solely for use on solemn occasions, such as coronations, were distinguished by great weight and richness of ornamentation. Personal crowns were made for wear during the final stages of the ceremony and the closing procession because St Edward's Crown, as a relic, had to be returned to the custody of Westminster Abbey. Even the personal crown was too heavy for comfort, however. At Richard I's coronation, for example, the crown was supported over the King's head by two earls and Richard donned a lighter crown afterwards. A cap had to be worn inside these great crowns to ensure a close fit. The cap used inside Edward III's Ryche Crowne was made of silk and embroidered with five gold quatrefoils decorated with four small sapphires, seven small garnets and twenty-eight small pearls.

Much of the symbolism that came to be attached to crowns, and indeed to other items of regalia, was formulated by medieval ecclesiastics, who ensured that it accorded with the Christian Church's notions of kingship. The placing of the crown on the highest point of the king's body signifies that as a crown is more beautiful and perfect than all other ornaments, so a king must excel all others in virtue. His virtues must be as durable as the gold and precious stones used to fashion the crown. The circular shape of the crown, without beginning or end, represents the eternity that will be his if he remains virtuous. The life led by a king on earth should be worthy of a heavenly crown when he dies. He will reign with his crown in heaven if he competes for justice on earth.

The twin notions that the kings of England owe allegiance to no man and are responsible only to God are embodied in the imperial crown. In the fifteenth century the imperial nature of the authority of English kings would be symbolized in a crown resembling the emperor's.

The imperial crowns ensigned with a cross disappeared from English usage during the thirteenth and fourteenth centuries and reappeared again under Henry VI. The pious Henry, founder of Eton College and King's College, Cambridge, had 'a very great devotion to the Holy

Portraits, coins and effigies are unreliable so far as showing precise details of the crowns worn by English kings. However, they do indicate clearly the styles of head-ornaments current in various periods. The line illustrations displayed depict changing styles in head-ornaments between the eleventh and fifteenth centuries: 1 and 2, from coins of William the Conqueror; 3, Byzantine type from an effigy of Richard I, Rouen Cathedral; 4, from an effigy of Richard I, Fontevraud; 5, from effigies of Henry III and his daughter-in-law Eleanor of Castile in Westminster Abbey; 6, from an effigy of Edward II, Gloucester Cathedral; 7, from portraits of Richard II; 8, from an effigy of Henry IV in Canterbury Cathedral.

Cross', according to his confessor John Blakman. He is said to have preferred to have a series of signs of the cross set on his crown than the customary decorative fleurons.

In medieval times symbolic significance was also attached to the gold and gems of royal crowns. The crown used at the coronation of Judith, the wife of King Ethelwulf of Wessex, in 856 was referred to as a 'crown of spiritual gems'. In the coronation address, God was called upon to place the crown on her head so that 'whatever is signified by the splendour of gold and various colours of gems may ever shine forth in thy ways and in thy deeds'.

The twelve types of stone incorporated in William the Conqueror's imperial-style coronation crown, made for him by a Byzantine goldsmith with materials from the Levant, were undoubtedly chosen for their symbolism. The stones represented the twelve types that God commanded Moses to set in Aaron's breast-ornament, later known as the Urim and Thummim of the Jewish High Priest. Without attributing too precise a meaning to each of the twelve stones, it is possible to interpret William's choice as an invocation to God to look favourably on his rule.

The mystical and practical properties attributed to these stones were widely recognized during the Middle Ages. The sapphire, for example, the gem of gems, signified chastity, and for this reason as well as its celestial colour was worn by churchmen. Amethysts symbolized humility and also preserved the wearer from drunkeness. Jasper signified perfection; red sard the height of honour; chrysolite, good morals (and if set in gold, was especially valued as a protector against night fears and demons); beryl, sevenfold grace (also a guardian of marital love); emerald, the virtue of the faithful; chrysoprase, perfect charity; sardony, complete faith (and a preserver of modesty and chastity); chalcedony, the virtues of the simple-hearted (and giver of victory in a cause); topaz, contemplation; and jacinth, a life of spirituality. The ruby was thought to possess the virtues of all the other precious stones and invoked reverence and love towards the lord who wore it. It became the traditional stone for the monarch's coronation ring.

THE CORONATION CEREMONY AND THE CROWN JEWELS

For Charles II's coronation in 1661 it was decided to have two crowns made: a replacement for St Edward's Crown, the coronation crown, and an imperial or state crown. The origins of the new St Edward's Crown are not entirely clear-cut and free of conjecture. The gold used in the crown would appear to have been provided gratis, for no record of payment exists. One possible explanation is that the gold was obtained from the regalia allegedly made for Oliver Cromwell in 1656. If this is so, then it may be that the new St Edward's Crown contains gold from the ornament known as St Alfred's Crown, which was seized in 1649. A be-jewelled gold crown, a sceptre and an orb were displayed at the Protector's lying-in-state in 1658. The orb and the sceptre were among the funeral 'properties' specially made for the occasion. The crown, it would seem, was already in existence and it is this item which, it is argued, may have been made from items of regalia seized by the Commonwealth authorities and bought by Cromwell. This theory is supported by the fact that there is no note in the Mint's otherwise well-kept records to confirm that the original St Edward's Crown was indeed converted into coinage.

St Edward's Crown, with which Charles was actually crowned, was ornamented with hired jewels, which were taken out of their settings and returned to the goldsmith after the coronation. The crown of state, by contrast, which would be required by the King when he went to Parliament, was permanently set with mostly bought stones; 890 diamonds, 10 rubies, 18 sapphires, 21 emeralds and 549 pearls. This crown was one of the ornaments that Captain Blood and his accomplices almost succeeded in stealing from the Tower in 1671.

The custom of the monarch using one state crown for both coronation and state openings and prorogations of Parliament was broken by Queen Anne in 1702. She had several crowns made. From the coronation of George I in 1714

Although Oliver Cromwell declined Parliament's offer of the throne, his rule bore some of the hallmarks of a monarchy, especially at the end. Under the new written constitution of 1657, the 'Humble Petition and Advice', the Protector received the title 'His Highness' and the right to nominate his own successor. A regalia was said to have been made for him in 1656. An orb and sceptre and a be-jewelled crown were displayed with the Protector's body at his lying-in-state at Somerset House two year laer. After the Restoration, officials of the Jewel House premises in Whitehall stripped the effigy of its ornaments and later hung it out of the window with a rope round its neck. What happened to the ornaments subsequently is not known; they may have been fake and discarded without mention.

THE CORONATION CEREMONY AND THE CROWN JEWELS

27

THE CORONATION CEREMONY AND THE CROWN JEWELS

to that of George IV in 1821 it appears that a coronation/state crown, usually known as the Imperial State Crown, was set specially for the coronation, with hired stones (invariably diamonds), performing the dual function of St Edward's Crown and the State Crown. Afterwards the monarch reverted to a state crown set with the traditional coloured stones when attending Parliament.

Anne had found Charles II's crowns too heavy and a new coronation/state crown, set with hired brilliant- and rose-cut diamonds valued at £79,000, was made. St Edward's Crown, elaborately dressed with hired stones, was preserved as a symbol and probably borne in the walking procession before the Queen. The new state crown, which was not completed until several months after her coronation, was set with old jewels, a mixture of diamonds and coloured stones (including the 'Black Prince's Ruby'), taken from the Imperial State Crowns of Charles II and William III.

The pillage of stones from old ornaments, including crowns, to make a new ornament had been common practice since medieval times, especially if the latter was required in haste; the pearls for the small coronation crown of the ten-year-old Edward VI, for example, were taken from the caps and collars of his father, Henry VIII. This practice also extended to the frames. The carcass of George I's post-coronation state crown served as the basis for George II's diamond coronation/state crown in 1727.

George IV, like Queen Anne, was loath to part with his coronation/state crown and kept it for almost two years after his coronation in 1821. He had hoped initially that the crown would be set permanently with diamonds. Disappointed, he then tried to persuade the government to buy the crown outright but met with no success on that score either.

His successor, William IV, was more economy minded. William's coronation/state crown was George I's post-coronation state crown which George IV had had thoroughly refurbished and to which a very large sapphire had been added. William was unwilling to spend any money on refurbishing the regalia, even on relatively inexpensive tasks such as

St Edward's Crown is the coronation crown. The original St Edward's Crown was lost in 1649, together with the rest of the medieval regalia. The present St Edward's Crown was made for the coronation of Charles II in 1661. The tradition of crowning the monarch with this emblem has not been upheld by all monarchs since 1661. After William III's coronation in 1689 the crown was not used again in its traditional central role until the coronation of George V in 1911.

The crown was permanently set with semi-precious stones for George V's coronation. Garrard's, the Crown jewellers, removed all the paste stones from the antique enamelled mounts and replaced them with 27 tourmalines, 37 white topaz, 3 yellow topaz, 12 Cape rubies, 7 amethysts, 6 sapphires, 1 carbuncle (a cabochon garnet), 1 peridot, 2 jargoons, 1 spinel ruby, 1 garnet and 345 rose-cut aquamarines. In addition, the rows of imitation pearls were replaced with gold beads plated with platinum. The cost of Garrard's work on the crown, which included supplying a new velvet cap with ermine border, was £375.

The problem of fitting the crown to different shaped craniums is overcome by altering the size of the band or inserting a custom-made inner 'helmet' (a wire skeleton frame).

The total weight of the crown is 71 oz 14 dwt (2.04 kg); the height 11.9 in (30.2 cm).

altering the frame of the crown to fit his head; indeed, he had not even wanted a coronation. He made do with a padded cap provided by the royal hatter, Francis Cater. William was said to have endured severe toothache on the day of his coronation, made worse by having to balance on his head an ornament weighing some 7 pounds (troy).

The current Imperial State Crown is reckoned to be about the tenth manifestation since the Restoration. It was made in 1937 for the coronation of George VI as a consequence of the resumption of the practice of crowning the monarch with St Edward's crown. It is a replica of the crown made for Queen Victoria in 1838, which was permanently set with jewels so that it could serve as a state crown for the rest of her

The Crown of State, or Imperial State Crown, is the crown with which the monarch is normally invested during the Recess at the end of the coronation ceremony. It is also worn by, or carried before, the monarch at the opening and closing of Parliament. The present Imperial State Crown was made for the coronation of King George VI in 1937 and is almost a replica of Queen Victoria's coronation/state crown of 1838.

The crown is set with 2,868 diamonds, 17 sapphires, 11 emeralds and 269 pearls. In the front of the band is the large cushion-shaped brilliant known as Cullinan II or the 'Second Star of Africa', at 317.4 metric carats the second largest stone cut from the Cullinan diamond. In the corresponding position at the back of the band is the 104-carat Stuart Sapphire, an oval mixed-cut stone in a hexagonal gold mount set with 12 small diamonds, 6 table- and rose-cut variations and 6 brilliants. The openwork frieze linking the two stones contains 16 clusters, each comprising 8 step-cut emeralds and 8 sapphires. The front cross-pattée contains the 170-carat 'Black Prince's Ruby', which is not a genuine ruby at all but a pear-shaped cabochon red spinel. The stone was once worn as a pendant jewel, hence the small drill holes in it; one of these, in the top right-hand corner, is plugged with a small ruby. The 'Ruby' is thought to have come from the East, but no one knows for certain how it came into royal possession. In one of the many fanciful legends associated with it, Don Pedro the Cruel, the grandee of Castile, gave the stone to the Black Prince in 1369 as a token of the latter's victory at the battle of Najara. He had acquired it by murdering the Moorish King of Granada. If the gem did, in fact, come into the possession of the Prince via Pedro, the likelihood is that it was sold to him and not given as a present. The stone was also said to have been one of the balas-rubies worn by Henry V on his helmet at the battle of Agincourt. How the stone found its way back into royal possession at the Restoration is equally uncertain. The octagonal stone in the centre of the cross above the monde is St Edward's Sapphire, so-called because it is said to have once belonged in the ring of Edward the Confessor. The four large drop-shaped pearls suspended from diamond-set silver arms at the intersection of the crown's arches are known as 'Queen Elizabeth's Earrings'. The association is certainly erroneous. Two of the pearls may have been among the stones used for Charles II's state crown. The remaining pair were added in the nineteenth century during the course of renovation work on the crown.

Excluding the wire frame, cap of estate and ermine band, the crown weighs 32 oz 7 dwt (1.06 kg). Its height is 12.4 in (31.5 cm).

Overleaf: The acquisition of the Kohinur diamond by Queen Victoria excited a great deal of interest in Britain. Soon after its arrival from India the diamond was put on show at the Great Exhibition. Its appearance disappointed many, including the wife of the writer Thomas Carlyle, Jane, who described the stone as 'precisely like a bit of crystal the size and shape of the first joint of your thumb'. The stone was considered useless as an ornamental gem because of its many flaws and in 1852 the decision was taken to re-cut it as a brilliant. This operation reduced the stone to 105.602 carats, possibly to its detriment. In its new form the stone was fitted for attachment to a new circlet ordered by Victoria or for alternative wear as a large honeysuckle brooch. It is currently set in Queen Elizabeth the Queen Mother's crown.

THE CORONATION CEREMONY AND THE CROWN JEWELS

Many stones in crowns made since the Restoration have a special interest of their own. In the case of the Kohinur diamond (opposite) a long and colourful history — much of it unverifiable — has made it an object of wonder. The stone was given to Queen Victoria in the name of the deposed Maharaja of the Punjab, ten-year-old Duleep Singh, the last of the four acknowledged sons of Ranjit Singh, under the terms of the Treaty of Bhyrowal in 1849. Its origins are sketchy, but a diamond thought to be Kohinur is mentioned in the memoirs of Babur (1483–1530), the first moghul ruler in India. According to Babur (seen at right in the background illustration), the diamond was acquired by Ala-ed-Din, Sultan of Delhi, during his conquests of the Deccan and Gujerat at the end of the thirteenth century. At this time the diamond weighed about 186 old carats and had a value equivalent to half of the daily expense of the entire world. Babur received the diamond as part of the tribute due to him after his conquest of Delhi and Agra.

The name Kohinur (meaning 'mountain of light') is said to have been given to the stone by the Persian leader Nadir Shah. It came into his possession via the last mogul emperor, Mohammed Shah, whom he vanquished in 1738. Nadir knew that his defeated enemy kept a large diamond in his headgear and tricked him into parting with it by insisting upon exchanging turbans. When Nadir first set eyes on the diamond, so the story runs, he exclaimed that it was like a mountain of light, thus giving it its name. Nadir was assassinated some nine years later, at which point the stone was taken from Persia to Afghanistan, in the possession of the Durani dynasty, and eventually back again to India. The Kohinur was extorted from the deposed ruler of Afghanistan, Shah Shuja, by the Indian prince in whose house he had sought sanctuary, Ranjit Singh.

Despite his own experience and the fact that the Kohinur had never, so it seems, changed hands other than by means of war, murder, usurpation and maiming, Shah Shuja declared that it brought good luck to whoever possessed it. Others thought that the stone brought bad luck to its male possessors, and this encouraged a belief that it never brought ill-fortune to women. Be this as it may, since the Kohinur's arrival in England in 1850 the stone has been worn only by queens-regnant and consort.

life; some of the jewels were taken from George I's crown, others were bought specially. This was subsequently used for the same purpose by her son, grandson and great-grandson, until it was broken up in 1937.

The new St Edward's Crown made for Charles II was not permanently set with jewels until 1911, bringing to an end the centuries-old practice of exchanging the fake jewels for real ones at times of coronation. The decision to reset the crown reflects its enhanced status. Charles II, James II and William III were all crowned with St Edward's Crown. Thereafter, however, until the accession of Edward VII in 1902 there seems to have been a diminution in its significance, at least in the eyes of some monarchs, and in its role in the coronation. For the coronations of George IV and William IV, for example, the crown was not dressed with real stones but appeared in its non-ceremonial state, ornamented with white and coloured pastes. The crown's role in the ceremony was shortened in 1831, when it was decided to abolish the traditional procession from Westminster Hall to the Abbey on the morning of the ceremony. The crown was not used at all for Queen Victoria's coronation in 1838.

All monarchs since Victoria have expressed a desire to be crowned with this great symbol of kingly power, beginning with Edward VII in 1902. Unfortunately, illness prevented Edward from carrying out his intention. He was not fully recovered from an operation for appendicitis and it was decided that he should wear his mother's lighter crown instead.

The refurbishment of the crown for the coronation of George V in 1911 included, in addition to the permanent setting of real stones, a remodelled band to fit the narrowness of his head; a characteristic inherited, it seems, from his mother, Queen Alexandra. This resulted in a further paring down of the crown's original weight of 82 ounces to 71 ounces (troy).

The bands of all crowns since the time of William III have been an oval shape; previously they were round. The problem of fitting the crown to heads of different sizes may be solved by either altering the band or fitting a shaped cap inside the crown, as in the case of William IV.

Opposite: Queen Elizabeth the Queen Mother's crown was made by Garrard's in 1937 for the coronation of George VI. The overall silhouette of the crown includes details reinterpreted from Queen Mary's crown of 1911, most strikingly the scrolling terminals of the half-arches on which the monde rests, the stylish profile of the crosses and the use of a drop-shaped diamond on the cross above the monde. Most of the crown's 2,800 diamonds were removed from the Regal Circlet remade for Queen Victoria in 1858. The 17.34-carat diamond set in the frieze below the Kohinur was given to Queen Victoria in 1856 by Abdul Mejdid, the Sultan of Turkey; it occupied the same position on Victoria's Regal Circlet. The stone on the cross above the monde is a rock crystal replica of a diamond from the Lahore Treasury. The Kohinur was taken from Queen Mary's crown and stripped of its rose-cut diamond frame to fit on the front cross. After the 1937 coronation, Queen Elizabeth wore the crown in circlet form when she accompanied King George VI to state openings of Parliament.

THE CORONATION CEREMONY AND THE CROWN JEWELS

Head Ornaments for Queen-Consorts

The crown ordered for the coronation of Queen Mary in 1911 was inspired by Queen Alexandra's crown, regarded as a miracle of construction because it weighed less than 23 oz when mounted with 3,668 diamonds. Queen Mary's crown contains 2,200 or so diamonds and weighs 22.85 oz (.59 kg). In the front of the band is a detachable rock crystal replica of Cullinan IV, a cushion-shaped brilliant of 63.6 carats. The front cross is set with a detachable rock crystal replica of the Kohinur. At the centre of the cross-pattée is a rock crystal replica of the 94.4 carat Cullinan III.

The first full account of a queen's coronation is that of Eleanor of Provence in 1236. From the late fourteenth century and possibly before, the crown worn by a queen for the opening procession of her coronation was traditionally given by the king. Isabelle of France received from Richard II on her coronation day a rich circlet of jewelled gold set with precious stones. For her coronation in 1509 Henry VIII's first wife, Catherine of Aragon, was given a circlet of gold set with diamonds and balas-rubies in rose motifs. The rose, a symbol of joy, was also a Tudor ensign.

A queen's crown was added to the regalia held at Westminster in the late fourteenth century. Very little is known of this crown, which subsequently came to be called Queen Edith's Crown – after the wife of Edward the Confessor – and regarded as the counterpart to St Edward's Crown. However, so far as can be ascertained, there was never a tradition of crowning queen-consorts with an hereditary crown.

The first crowns made for a queen-consort after the Restoration and included in the regalia were a coronation crown and a state crown for Mary of Modena, the wife of James II; Charles II was unmarried at the time of his coronation in 1661. Both were small and sat on top of her head. The cost of the 38 very large diamonds, 523 great and small diamonds and 129 large pearls in the state crown was the subject of much speculation. Gossip raised their combined value – estimated officially at £35,000 – well above £200,000. The crowns were dressed with a lavish mixture of jewels for the coronation of Mary II in 1689. A fortnight later they were reset with false stones for display in the Tower.

After Mary's coronation both crowns – or, more correctly, their frames – are known to have been used at two further coronations, those of the queen-consorts Wilhelmina Caroline, in 1727, and Charlotte, in 1760, although it is conceivable that Queen Adelaide was crowned with one of them in 1831. The coronation crown was sent for repair to the workshop of the royal goldsmiths, Rundell, Bridge and Rundell, in the 1830s and never returned to the Tower. It was probably sold unrecognized when the firm ceased trading in 1842. The crown came to light over one hundred years later, in 1956, at which point it was acquired by the Museum of London.

In addition to her coronation and state crowns, Mary of Modena also had a diadem made for her coronation in 1685. This circlet was worn before her anointing. Mary II, joint-sovereign with William III, wore the same diadem in her coronation procession in 1689. It is likely that the diadem was re-dressed with rose-cut pastes at the beginning of the eighteenth

Mary of Modena's State Crown and diadem were the first head ornaments made for the coronation of a queen-consort after the Restoration. Both ornaments fell into disrepair through disuse at the end of the eighteenth century. The old pastes in both ornaments were eventually replaced with rock crystals (quartzes) and the imitation pearls with cultured pearls.

The crown weighs 23 oz (.7 kg) and is 7½ in (19 cm) high; the diadem weighs 14.8 oz (.3 kg) and is 3 in (8 cm) high.

The design of the small crown made for Queen Victoria in 1870 to wear on top of her widow's cap was probably based on that of Queen Charlotte's nuptial crown. The small crown became closely identified with the Queen; weighing only 5.11 oz (.16 kg), it was light and comfortable to wear. It was added to the regalia in 1937, although it has never been used at a coronation ceremony.

century. These were eventually replaced by rock crystal (quartz). Since then only the consorts of George II and George III, Wilhelmina Caroline and Charlotte, may have worn the diadem in the procession at their coronations. William IV's wife, Adelaide, may also have worn the same ornament. As the old walking procession had been abolished, she presumably assumed it on arrival at the Abbey.

In 1939 Mary of Modena's State Crown and her diadem were refurbished and reset with cultured pearls; her orb also received attention at this time. It had not been used for a long time and many of its imitation pearls were discoloured, broken or lost.

The Sceptre, Staff or Rod

The sceptre is a symbol of the royal power of command and also a reminder to the sovereign of the importance of justice. The monarch must be committed to this in order to gain a heavenly crown. Together with the crown, the sceptre was one of the two main ensigns of royalty in the medieval period. The consecration of Charles the Bald, the king of West Francia, in Orleans in 848 marked the first recorded appearance of the sceptre as an item of coronation ornament. In 876, shortly after his coronation as emperor, Charles would use both a sceptre and a long staff as ensigns.

The rod or staff, thought to derive from the shepherd's staff or crook, signifies the pastoral aspect of the kingly office. The ancient Egyptians and people of the Near East were the first to utilize it as a symbol of royal power. For the Romans, who came to use it later, the rod denoted magistracy. Constantine gave the rod Christian significance by setting a cross on the end. However, it would seem that the Byzantines regarded the rod as an imperial ornament and not as an item of regalia to be used at the coronation of their emperors.

A sceptre and rod (or staff) are thought to have been royal ensigns in England from at least as early as the ninth century. The earliest orders for the coronation ceremony, which date from this time, call for the delivery of both items. Anglo-Saxon coins include representations of sceptres, and King Edgar is known to have carried a sceptre on ceremonial occasions prior to his coronation and anointing at Bath in 973.

St Edward's regalia included a sceptre and rod or staff, but there is little firm evidence of their form. The sceptre is thought to have been of gold with a cross on top and set with gems and pearls. Byzantine influence is suggested by the four pendants of pearls that are said to have hung from the head of the sceptre and a cross on the top. Coins of Edward the Confessor issued in 1057 show a long sceptre topped with a cross. The rod or staff of St Edward was in effect a long walking staff with a pike at the bottom end. It was of wood plated at the top with gold and lower down with silver-gilt. Edward was known to have used a long staff

This unusual representation, from the Bayeux Tapestry, is thought to reflect historical reality. Edward the Confessor is shown seated on a state stool holding a long staff with a pike at the end and a knob at the top. The staff appears to be held by the King as an everyday ensign of authority, as opposed to the ceremonial sceptre. The staff in St Edward's regalia may have been a genuine relic of the Confessor. Its first certain appearance in the coronation ceremony came in 1483. On this occasion, the coronation of Richard III, the staff was borne after the spurs in the opening procession. The evidence suggests that by 1540 the staff had also become an ensign handed to the king on formal visits to the Abbey in token of the Confessor's role as founder.

Above: *King Edward VII holding the Sceptre with Cross originally made for the coronation of Charles II in 1661. It is not known whether the remade St Edward's sceptre, with its cross surmounting an orb, reproduces a feature of the Confessor's original sceptre. This long sceptre surmounted by a cross appeared for the first time on the Confessor's coins in 1057. Edward VII was the last monarch to use the sceptre before the diamond known as Cullinan I was inserted in the head.*

Below left: *The world's largest cut diamond, Cullinan I, was set in the head of the Sceptre with Cross in 1910. The diamond is a segment from the 3,106-carat rough stone discovered in South Africa's Premier goldmine in 1905. The Transvaal government made a gift of the stone to King Edward VII. The cutting of the diamond – the largest gem-quality rough diamond ever found – in 1908 yielded two large stones (Cullinan I and II) and an assortment of smaller gems.*

When free of its settings the colourless Cullinan I weighs 530.2 carats. Its dimensions are 58.9 mm (length) × 45.4 mm (width) × 27.7 mm (depth). The stone is set in a large hinged heart-shaped white-enamelled frame beneath the monde.

40

(Baculus) as an everyday royal ensign. The St Edward's Staff or Rod that came to play a role in the coronation procession was not a royal ensign but a relic borne because of its association with the sainted King. By the time of the coronation of Charles I, it had become an ensign delivered to the king on entering Westminster Abbey as a symbolic reference to the Confessor's role as its second founder. Charles carried the Staff up the nave but, recognizing that it had no role in the ceremony, relinquished it when he reached the 'theatre'.

Two rods briefly associated with the personal regalia of English kings were those associated with Moses, the first Jewish leader, and Aaron, the first Jewish high priest. Both rods of Moses and Aaron were valued as relics by medieval kings and emperors for their biblical associations. The first represented the wooden rod that Moses used to part the Red Sea, and with which he made the bitter waters of the desert sweet and struck water from the rock; the second represented the rod that had flowered to signify God's preference for Aaron as high priest and was then preserved in the tabernacle. The only coronation ceremony in which both rods are known for sure to have appeared is that of Henry VI in 1422, when they were carried in the procession. The notion, implicit in these symbols, was that of princely and priestly power deriving from God.

The sceptre and rod were not delivered to the queen at coronations until the fourteenth century. Both ornaments were topped with a dove with its wings displayed, symbolizing the quality of gentleness attributed to a queen. The choice of material for the sceptre of a medieval queen signified her inferiority in rank to a king. It was

Far left: The Sceptre with Cross and Sceptre with Dove. Both are made of gold and decorated with champlevé enamel and stones. The Sceptre with Cross is set with 393 gemstones: 333 diamonds, 31 rubies, 15 emeralds, 7 sapphires, 6 spinels and 1 composite amethyst. The Sceptre with Dove is decorated with a total of 285 stones: 94 diamonds, 53 rubies, 10 emeralds, 4 sapphires and 3 spinels. The Sceptre with Cross is 36.5 in (92.2 cm) long and weighs 37.14 oz (1.17 kg). The Sceptre with Dove is significantly longer, at 43.5 in (110.2 cm), and weighs 37 oz (1.15 kg).

Left: St Edward's Staff is set aside on the altar after the opening procession and is not among the items of regalia delivered to the monarch. The present staff was supplied for the coronation of Charles II. Made of gold and decorated with friezes of chased acanthus leaves on a matted ground, it has a monde and cross at its head and a steel spike at its bottom. Apart from the addition of a strengthening collar, possibly in 1716, the staff has been little altered since 1661. The claim that the monde conceals a 'fragment of the true Cross' is certainly erroneous. The staff is 56 in (142 cm) long and weighs 55 oz 19 dwt (1.74 kg).

made of silver-gilt, the second most important precious metal after gold, the traditional material chosen for a king's sceptre.

A new St Edward's Staff was made for Charles II's coronation in 1661 to replace the original lost during the Commonwealth. The new ornament was borne in the walking procession and set aside on the altar but not delivered to the monarch. Two sceptres were made for Charles's coronation: one with a cross and one with a dove. The first, symbolizing the sovereign's temporal power under the cross, may also have been intended for Charles's use in Parliament. The second signifies the monarch's spiritual role, the dove representing the Holy Ghost, and is known by its traditional name of 'The Rod of Equity and Mercy'.

The regalia also includes a sceptre with dove made for Mary II, joint sovereign with her husband William III, a sceptre with cross for a queen consort and an ivory rod with dove for a queen consort. These last two were made for Mary of Modena in 1685. In Mary II's sceptre the wings of the dove are displayed, indicating a sovereign, not a consort. The item has only been used once, for Mary's coronation in 1689. It disappeared from view some time after 1768 until it was discovered on a shelf in an old cupboard in the Jewel House in 1814. It was repaired soon afterwards and re-enamelled.

The Orb

This ancient imperial ensign signified Roman rule over the whole world. In the fourth century the Emperor Theodosius I added a cross, thereby giving the orb Christian significance. Before the Fourth Crusade (1202–4) the orb was much used in Byzantine imperial portraiture, but it seems never to have become an actual imperial ornament. In the West, the orb was used as a purely pictorial emblem until the eleventh century when, it seems, Pope Benedict VIII had one made for the coronation of the Saxon Emperor Henry II in 1014. Not until the coronation of the Emperor Henry VI, however, is there firm evidence for the orb's actual use at an imperial coronation. Henry is said to have received the emblem from the Pope with the utmost suspicion because his acceptance of it

THE CORONATION CEREMONY AND THE CROWN JEWELS

THE CORONATION CEREMONY AND THE CROWN JEWELS

Orb-sceptres are first clearly mentioned in connection with the funeral rites for kings in the fourteenth century. At his coronation in 1377, Richard II is said to have received an orb-sceptre – similar to the one he is depicted holding here – in place of St Edward's sceptre.

could have been taken as a sign that the emperor's earthly power derived from the Church and not directly from God.

In England, too, the orb may not have been used as an actual item of regalia until several centuries after its introduction as a pictorial emblem. It became established as a royal ensign as a consequence of Edward the Confessor using it on his first seal. On this the Confessor is depicted holding a simple orb without a cross in his left hand. Harold followed Edward's example: in the Bayeux Tapestry he is shown sitting in majesty holding an orb surmounted with a cross. William the Conqueror is shown holding an orb-sceptre, a form of orb that would remain peculiar to the English monarchy. (The distinguishing characteristic of the orb-sceptre is that the cross is set on a stem instead of directly on the ball, as in a simple orb.) In later iconography the orb-sceptre is shown with decorative variations. On the second Great Seal of Richard I (1189), for example, the stem is long and floriated. The list given for St Edward's regalia in 1359 does not include an orb of any kind, nor do any of the surviving earlier lists and inventories of the regalia. It is uncertain, therefore, whether orbs were actually made before the later fourteenth century. Earlier representations may have been simply pictorial creations which attempted to combine the orb, sceptre, and, in some instances, the rod into a single ensign.

The orb is thought to have been introduced into the English regalia about the same time as the reintroduction of the imperial crown, during the reign of either Henry V or Henry VI, in the fifteenth century, and probably for the same reason – to underline the king's imperial status. The orb that belonged to Henry VIII is the first English ornament of this type for which there is a description. The orb was delivered to the Tudor kings and queens, beginning with Henry VIII, but not to the early Stuarts, James I and Charles I, both of whom used the original medieval coronation order, *Liber Regalis*, which omits it. The orb was deposited with the Westminster regalia in the seventeenth century, probably immediately after the coronation of Charles I in 1625, and was lost with most of the other items of regalia in 1649.

Charles II was very keen to have 'A Ball and Crosse of Gold' for his coronation and it was the second item on his list of ornaments required for the ceremony. The new orb made for his coronation weighed over 42 ounces (troy) and was significantly larger than the one lost in 1649, which had weighed slightly over 17 ounces (troy). The sovereign's orb was damaged during Captain Blood's unsuccessful attempt to steal the Crown Jewels from the Tower in 1671.

Neither the orb nor the Sceptre with Dove made for Mary II has since been used at a coronation. The gold orb was set with hired jewels and re-dressed later with imitation and synthetic stones. It weighs 34 oz 6 dwt (1.07 kg) and is 5.75 in (14.6 cm) in diameter. The gold and silver Sceptre with Dove contains 274 gemstones and 9 settings from which the stones are missing. The majority of the stones are colourless, probably quartz with some sapphire. The sceptre is 39.5 in (100.4 cm) long and weighs 33.9 oz (1.05 kg).

Below right: *This illustration from an early eleventh-century translation of parts of the Old Testament depicts a king, as judge, ordering the execution of an errant subject.*

Below left: *One of the swords borne before the monarch at early medieval coronations may have represented the duchy of Normandy, which Geoffrey Plantagenet (shown here) had secured for his heir, the future Henry II of England.*

The orb made for Mary II's joint-coronation with her husband William III in 1689 has not been used in a coronation ceremony since. It was unset afterwards and subsequently dressed with imitation stones for public viewing. Throughout the nineteenth century the public were given to understand that the fake stones adorning the orb were precious. In 1939 the ornament was reset with cultured pearls.

The Swords

The sword symbolizes the monarch's authority and his role as a leader in war. It has been suggested that the delivery of a sword in the coronation ritual has its origin in the inauguration of the pagan Germanic warrior tribes. However, although it was customary for their kings to wear a helmet and sword at their inaugurations, there is no direct evidence to support the notion that delivery of a sword formed part of the ceremony. Its introduction into the coronation ceremony is probably an example of the early Church's common practice of Christianizing pagan customs. The Church became involved in the ritual of delivery in 823 at the coronation of the Carolingian Emperor Lothar, who was girded with a sword by the Pope. Previously the Emperor Charlemagne had on two separate occasions used the delivery of a sword to symbolize the attainment of manhood and the ceding of authority. He had girded his son Louis the Pious in 781 when he gave him the

THE CORONATION CEREMONY AND THE CROWN JEWELS

kingdom of Aquitaine and again, in 791, to mark the boy's thirteenth birthday, the threshold of adolescence.

The two symbolic functions attaching to the sword in the English coronation ritual are the defence of the Church and the defence of the people. The delivery of the sword symbolizes the transference of the kingdom into the care of the king. Early representations of English kings commonly show the enthroned ruler holding an erect sword together with a sceptre or staff or orb. From early times the sword has been regarded as one of the most potent symbols of royal power, on a par with the crown and sceptre. To hold or carry the sword of a king was one of the ways by which great men acknowledged their dependence and vassalage. Such was the prestige of the sword as an ensign that magnates vied with each other for the honour of performing this service at coronation. In the medieval period, and especially in the age of chivalry during the

The present Sword of State (top) *was made in 1678 and has been used at the coronations of all monarchs from George IV onwards and possibly from as early as that of James II. The sword weighs 83 oz (2.58 kg) and the scabbard 34 oz (1.06 kg). The Swords of Temporal and Spiritual Justice and of Mercy (Curtana) did not become a permanent part of the regalia until after the coronation of Charles I in 1626. The present swords date to the early part of the seventeenth century.*

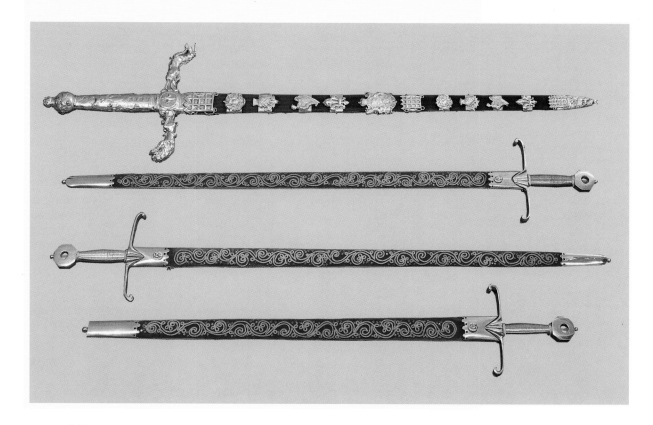

King George V, Queen Mary and other members of the royal family attending a Thanksgiving Service at Westerminster Abbey in 1935. The Sword of State (held at right), for centuries a visible symbol of the royal presence, is nowadays normally in evidence only at the annual opening of Parliament. The honour of bearing it on these occasions is usually bestowed on a high-ranking officer from one of the armed services.

twelfth and thirteenth centuries, swords were prized and collected by kings as well as noblemen for their associations with famous chivalric champions. King John, for example, owned Curtein, or Curtana, the sword of the knight Tristram. Part of Curtana's blade was missing, lost during Tristram's bloody fight with Morhaut, champion of Ireland. This mighty sword was, according to legend, given by Charlemagne to the chivalric champion Ogier the Dane. It figured in English coronations in the thirteenth century and was regarded for some time as the principal sword of English monarchs. Elizabeth I, for example, was girded with Curtana. The Sword of Mercy used in the modern coronation ceremony is called the Curtana and has the characteristic truncated blade which the name suggests, the lack of a point symbolizing the mercy that ought to temper the sharpness of royal justice.

The swords with which medieval kings were invested at their coronations were probably personal, weapons with which they went out and fought battles. By the fifteenth century it had become usual practice to provide a new sword for each coronation, although there had been periods when some swords were kept as part of a permanent regalia. From an early date, probably Anglo-Saxon times, it seems certain that this investiture was symbolized at other formal occasions by a sword that was either carried by the monarch or by a sword-bearer. The sword was a visible symbol of the royal presence and formal proceedings involving the monarch could not be held until it was displayed. The practice gradually came to an end in the second half of the eighteenth century, probably

THE CORONATION CEREMONY AND THE CROWN JEWELS

during the reign of George III, except for royal attendances at the Houses of Parliament and for the ceremony of making knights. The sword's use is now normally confined to the annual opening of Parliament, though it is very occasionally carried before the monarch on other occasions; for example, at the investiture of the Prince of Wales in 1969. Any sword carried before the monarch officially is called the Sword of State.

Two Swords of State were made at the Restoration. One is the Irish Sword of State, which is now shown with the Crown Jewels. The other was the main Sword of State. Little is known about its appearance or its whereabouts after Charles's coronation. The last record of it was in 1770. The present Sword of State was made in 1678 and has been used at the coronations of all monarchs from George IV onwards and possibly from as early as that of James II.

The one true coronation sword is the Sword of Offering, the sword with which the monarch is invested. All other swords carried before the monarch are manifestations of it. Until the coronation of George V in 1911 the Sword of Offering was always, in theory, provided personally by the monarch and paid for out of his or her own pocket. In 1903 a permanent Sword of Offering was introduced into the Jewel House for use at all coronations. The jewel-encrusted sword had been made at a cost of £5,088 for the coronation of George IV in 1821 when it was described as an 'elegant brilliant sword of state'. Many articles of jewellery in the King's possession were broken up for use in the new sword, which represented a magnificent departure from those made for his immediate predecessors — Queen Anne, George I, II and III — who were presented with items of base metal costing less than two pounds apiece.

The original practice was for the Sword of Offering to be carried before the monarch in the procession from Westminster Hall and throughout the proceedings until the time came for it to be delivered. The bearer then placed the sword on the altar, where it was blessed before being girded on the monarch. After girding, the monarch offered the sword at the altar, from where the original bearer immediately redeemed it on payment of 100 new shillings. The sword was then carried unsheathed during the rest of the proceedings. A change from this procedure was first recorded at the coronation of Charles I and became the norm from that of Queen Anne onwards. A Sword of State is now borne in the early part of the proceedings and then exchanged for a separate, smaller and more manageable Sword of Offering for the blessing and girding. The Sword of Offering is borne during the rest of the ceremony unsheathed.

In addition to the Sword of State/Sword of Offering, three other swords are carried before the monarch during the service and procession. These swords, which symbolize different aspects of the Sword of Offering, are called the Swords of Temporal and Spiritual Justice and the Sword of Mercy (Curtana). The custom of bearing four swords in the opening procession was probably initiated by Henry IV in 1399; previously three swords were borne. They are probably survivors of the old regalia used at Charles I's coronation, having no intrinsic value.

The Spurs

The introduction of spurs into the English coronation ceremony is likely to have been inspired by the ritual for making a knight, which included the buckling of spurs to his heels. The knighting of Geoffrey of Anjou at Rouen in 1128 was the first recorded instance of the appearance of spurs at a ceremony of knighthood. The monarch's donning of spurs had the same symbolic meaning as girding on the coronation sword: the assumption of earthly power and leadership in war. Romantic chivalrous sentiment may have influenced the decision to include spurs among the ornaments delivered at coronation. The first recorded use of spurs at a coronation was in 1189, for Richard I, although they had in all probability already figured in the coronation of the younger Henry, son and heir of Henry II, in 1170.

The first pair of spurs known to be regarded as a permanent part of the regalia were the so-called St Edward's Spurs. Their origins are unknown, but their first recorded use was at the coronation of Henry IV in 1399, and they were used regularly thereafter until their destruction by the Commonwealth in 1649. They were described in 1399 as being of the type known as prick spurs – with single goads instead of rowels – which had gone out of fashion some 50 years previously. The probability is, therefore, that they date from before the mid-fourteenth century, though the association with Edward the Confessor was certainly erroneous.

Opposite: The present Sword of Offering, the true coronation sword, was made for the coronation of George IV in 1821. It comprises a steel blade mounted in gold and set with precious stones; the gold-covered leather scabbard is also set with jewels, some 1,251 diamonds, 16 rubies, 2 sapphires and 2 turquoises. The actual sword is set with 2,141 diamonds, 12 emeralds and 4 rubies.

The introduction of spurs among the ornaments delivered at coronation may have been prompted by the similar chivalric sentiment that brought the sword Curtana into the opening procession. The gold spurs that had become a feature of the coronation regalia by 1189 symbolized knighthood, and their use in the coronation ritual derived directly from the ceremony of creating a knight.

The present gold spurs were made for the coronation of Charles II. They are of a type known as a prick spur, the earliest form of spur and the only type available in the time of Edward the Confessor; contrast with the later rowel spur shown in the top illustration.

Bracelets or armills are ancient biblical symbols of regality. They have been used as royal insignia since the twelfth century. The bracelets lost at the Interregnum were jewelled. Their replacements, made for the coronation of Charles II, are of enamelled gold with herringbone and floral decoration and lined with red velvet.

Opposite: Queen Elizabeth II is one of the few monarchs since the Restoration to have been invested with the bracelets. A new pair of plain gold bracelets was made for her coronation in 1953 as a symbol of the British Commonwealth of Nations. Each bracelet is fitted with an invisible hinge and a spring catch operated by a cast Tudor rose.

The new spurs made for Charles II's coronation in 1661 are in the present regalia. Made of gold, they too are prick spurs. They have not undergone any fundamental change since 1661, apart from the substitution of new buckles and attachments for the leather for the coronation of George IV in 1821. They have been called St George's Spurs since the late nineteenth century.

 ### The Bracelets (Armillas)

These items have a long history as royal ornaments in the East, as well as among the Germans, Scandinavians and Anglo-Saxons; the Romans, by contrast, considered them suitable only for women. In their original form they were probably worn around the arm rather than the wrists.

Bracelets (armillas) are first required in the new English coronation order introduced during the twelfth century, as a result of the influence of the orders for the imperial coronation ceremony. There was biblical precedent for the use of bracelets in the inauguration of a king: in the first book of Samuel, for example, David is brought the bracelets and diadem worn by Saul at his death. The history of bracelets in the medieval period is unclear because of a confusion in terminology which appears to have occurred in Westminster Abbey. The bracelets seem to have been mistaken for the stole, also used in the ceremony. The stole, which came to be known as the armil, was a band of material, probably of silk interwoven with gold thread, worn across the sovereign's shoulders. The loose ends hung down to the elbows, to which they were fastened with silk laces.

Bracelets in the true sense of bejewelled items worn on the wrists did not disappear from the royal regalia and they continued to play a part in the coronation ceremony, albeit sporadically. There is a possibility, for instance, that they were delivered to Richard II. There is no evidence of their use at Charles II's coronation, although a pair of oval gold bracelets lined with

velvet was made for the occasion, nor of their use at the accession ceremonies of his successors until 1727. On that occasion, the coronation of George II, the bracelets were taken to Westminster Abbey but it is not certain that the king was actually invested with them.

A new pair of bracelets was presented for the coronation of Elizabeth II in 1953 by the governments of the United Kingdom, Canada, Australia, New Zealand, South Africa, Pakistan, Ceylon and Southern Rhodesia. Elizabeth was the first monarch for some considerable time to be invested with bracelets at her coronation. The Keeper of the Jewel House carried these emblems at the ceremony, following a precedent established in the sixteenth century at the coronation of Edward VI.

In the Middle Ages the bracelets or armillas were confused with the stole by the monks of Westminster. This item is among the liturgical vestments with which the sovereign is invested at coronation.

The Ring

The ring is a symbol of faith, denoted by its unbroken form. It has been a constant feature of English coronations since the tenth century and was originally delivered in imitation of the ecclesiastical practice of delivering a ring to bishops on their consecration.

A ring removed from Edward the Confessor's body at his second translation in 1163 was received by Edward III at his coronation in 1327, but the practice of using this ring did not become established. The ring appears to have been supplied by each king for his own coronation. Richard II tried to establish his own ring as the hereditary coronation ring by stipulating that on his death it should be kept permanently at the Confessor's shrine for his successors to wear at their coronations.

The practice of having a personal ring prevented the seizure of Charles I's coronation ring by the Commonwealth authorities in 1649. This ring remained in the possession of the Stuart family on the Continent until 1807 when, on the death of James II's grandson, Cardinal Henry of York (or Henry IX), it was returned to Britain. It now forms part of the Scottish Crown Jewels in Edinburgh.

The ruby, the lordliest and most beautiful of precious stones, became the traditional stone for coronation rings. The earliest coronation ring known with certainty to have been set with a ruby was worn by Henry III at his coronation in 1220. The ring for George IV's coronation in 1821 departed from this precedent, being made with a large sapphire head overlaid with a ruby cross and bordered by diamonds.

The rings in the present regalia are the sovereign's ring (King William IV's coronation ring), the queen consort's coronation ring (Queen Adelaide's coronation ring), both made in 1831, and Queen Victoria's coronation ring, made in 1838, which is a miniature version of William IV's ring. Queen Adelaide bequeathed her ring and William IV's to Queen Victoria at her death in 1849. Victoria left them to the Crown in 1901, together with her own.

The present sovereign's ring (top) was made for the coronation of William IV in 1831. It weighs 84.45 carats and is set with a large sapphire (15.2 × 12.2 × 7.4 mm) surrounded by 14 diamonds; 2 more diamonds decorate the shank and 5 rubies are clear-set on the sapphire in the form of a cross. All sovereigns from Edward VII onwards have used this ring.

Queen Victoria's ring (middle) is a miniature version of William IV's coronation ring. It weighs 42.74 carats and is set with a large sapphire (14.6 × 13.2 × 8.5 mm) surrounded by 20 diamonds; 5 rubies are clear-set on the sapphire in the form of a cross and 31 diamonds decorate the shank (one diamond is missing).

The queen consort's coronation ring (bottom) was made for Queen Adelaide's use at the coronation of her husband, William IV, in 1831. It weighs 50.15 carats and is set with a large ruby (12.5 × 9.0 × 5.9 mm) surrounded by 14 diamonds; 14 rubies are set in the shank. The ring has been worn by Queens Alexandra, Mary and Queen Elizabeth the Queen Mother.

All three rings were left to the Crown in 1901, a bequest of Queen Victoria, and were deposited with the other regalia in the Tower by George V in 1919.

The Devices of Ritual

THE MODERN CORONATION CEREMONY has evolved from beginnings that are over one thousand years old. Despite many changes the ritual's early medieval origins are still in evidence beneath the influences of subsequent history. Our knowledge of the way in which the ceremony has changed over the centuries derives from two main sources: the orders devised for the ceremony, and eye-witness accounts of what actually occurred. Additional evidence in the form of accounts for the expenses incurred for various coronations is available from the late fifteenth century onwards. The clergy were from the first the main devisers and organizers of the ceremony, initially drawing on ceremonials that had already been formulated for consecrating bishops and later borrowing and adapting orders composed for other coronations. One of the most important early sources of information on coronation ritual tapped by these clerics was West Francia (now France), the western part of the divided empire of Charlemagne's descendants, and many of the ideas formulated there found their way into the ceremonials developed for English kings. In the twelfth century the East Frankish or German ritual exercised the major influence on English practice.

The order used for the coronation of King Ethelred in 978 was the first to establish clearly the division of the coronation service into election, oath, anointing, delivery of insignia and blessing. (The earliest formulary, devised at the end of the ninth century, had simply consisted of a set of prayers invoking God's help to make the king virtuous and pious throughout his reign. The king was then anointed, enthroned and acclaimed but he did not receive insignia.) The order devised for Ethelred's coronation was used for his successors until c. 1100, although modified and adapted to suit circumstances and individual preferences rather than remaining as sacrosanct model texts adhered to slavishly; at least five versions of the order originally devised for Ethelred are known to exist.

The Archbishop of Canterbury and his entourage, in consultation with the royal court, were probably responsible for drawing up the coronation orders of the late tenth to thirteenth centuries; the authorship of the earliest formulary, dating from c. 880, is not known. By the time the line of the kings of Kent came to an end in 825, Canterbury had shrewdly redirected its loyalty to the rulers of the kingdom of Wessex who, by defeating both Mercia and Northumbria, established themselves as the kings of all England. In 1072 a Church Council confirmed the Archbishop as the most important primate in England, thus officially settling a long-running dispute between York and Canterbury for this distinction. Even after the decision, York would at times continue to press its claim. Canterbury responded by producing a series of forged papal bulls in the early twelfth century, confirming its position as primatial see and claiming for itself the sole right to ordain and crown the kings of England.

In the early consecration rituals the custom seems to have been for all the bishops present to participate; in 796 Eardwulf of Northumbria, for example, seems to have been consecrated by the Archbishop of York and also the Bishops of Hexham, Whithorn and Lindisfarne. In the tenth and eleventh centuries the usual practice was for both York and Canterbury to take part in the coronation of Anglo-Saxon kings, although with Canterbury acting as the senior of the two. Canterbury's primacy was already recognized in court circles for some time before the decision of 1072: for example, in 1037 Queen Emma, Canute's wife, deemed it unlawful for anyone other than the Archbishop of Canterbury to lead a king to the throne. William the Conqueror would almost certainly have been crowned by the Archbishop of Canterbury and not the Archbishop of York had the former, Stigand, not been in disgrace at the time. On the few occasions when Canterbury has not officiated at coronations, there have always been special circumstances.

In 1220 Henry III began the transformation of Edward the Confessor's Norman minster at Westminster into a church that would serve as both a coronation church and a place of royal burial. The first change was the addition of a Lady Chapel. He donated the cost of the gold spurs he had received at his recent coronation to the building fund. Liturgical plate and silver were among the gifts he would make to the Abbey during his reign.

From the reign of Henry III (1216–72) responsibility for the devising of orders for coronation was gradually taken over by the monks of Westminster Abbey, which by this time had become the unquestioned coronation church of English kings. Before 1066 there had been no single place of coronation, and other churches had fulfilled the function equally well. Several tenth-century Anglo-Saxon kings had chosen the royal chapel at Kingston-upon-Thames as their coronation venue; Athelstan (925) and Ethelred the Unready (978), for example. (The church was probably that of All Hallows, replaced about 1120 by the Norman church of All Saints, now the parish church of Kingston.) The royal chapel at Bath was the choice of Edgar in 973, possibly because the city's Roman associations provided an appropriately imperial setting. The summons issued to call all the archbishops, bishops, great abbots and abbesses, dukes, prefects and judges to Bath is the first of which we have a record.

THE CORONATION CEREMONY AND THE CROWN JEWELS

Precedent was an important factor in a king's choice of coronation church. Winchester was chosen by Edward the Confessor because two of his predecessors, Canute and his son Hardacanute, were buried there. William the Conqueror would choose Westminster Abbey because it was the Confessor's last resting place, and the Norman usurper wanted to legitimize his new line by forging a connection between himself and a revered predecessor. William's selection of Westminster Palace as his main royal residence would influence his Norman successors' choice of the Abbey as their coronation church, for the two were conveniently adjacent to each other. By the time of Osbert of Clare's energetic campaign to establish the Abbey as the sole place of coronation, in the 1130s, it had already achieved that status in practice.

As much significance would come to be attached to the place of coronation as to the ceremony itself. Henry III would feel so uneasy about his hasty coronation at Gloucester in 1216 – forced on him by the necessity of warding off a dual threat to his claim from rebel barons and invading French forces – that he referred to his second coronation in Westminster Abbey some four years later as his first coronation. Henry would be responsible for reconstructing the Abbey along the lines of Rheims cathedral, for centuries the coronation church of French kings, and for encouraging the cult of the Confessor. The relics of the sainted king were removed in 1269 from their original place of burial to a shrine at the end of St Edward's Chapel in the new Abbey.

The order for the coronation of Edward II in 1308 was probably drawn up by the monks of Westminster. Gradually the monks would devise for themselves and St Edward's regalia precise roles in the ceremony, Westminster would formally constitute itself master of ceremonies to the coronation with the compilation of the so-called Westminster Missal, written in 1383–4, and the *Liber Regalis*, devised a few years later. The Missal gives the services of the Mass for the year. The *Liber Regalis* describes the ceremonials for royal burials and coronations. These first complete guides to coronation ritual established Westminster as the sole authority in all matters concerning the coronation proceedings in the church. However, the royal court and its clerical advisers would continue to modify the ritual as they chose, despite Westminster's prescriptions. Henry VI (1422), for example, received the ornaments before being clothed in the robes of St Edward, an inversion of the order prescribed by the *Liber Regalis*, and was crowned twice with St Edward's Crown.

One important innovation of the coronation orders included in the *Liber Regalis* was the spiritual preparation demanded of the king prior to his coronation. The Abbot of Westminster played a central role in this, attending the monarch before the coronation to instruct him in its ceremonial aspects and also preparing him for anointing. Eight days after coronation the Abbot and his monks would now also perform the ceremony of dealbation (see page 97), a task previously reserved for bishops.

The Abbey and Palace of Westminster, c.1537. About 1243 the Confessor's original church (see illustration on page 14) was pulled down as far west as the nave and work begun on Henry III's sumptuous memorial to his sainted ancestor. The first Palace of Westminster was built for the Confessor and beginning with William the Conqueror was the home of the kings of England until 1512, when Henry VIII moved the Court to Whitehall Palace.

The eve of coronation acquired a ceremonial framework of its own. The day began with the Vigil Procession, a secular cavalcade from the Tower of London to Westminster Palace, which was held for almost every coronation between 1377 and 1661; epidemics of the plague forced its cancellation for the coronations of James I and Charles I.

The first and last Vigil Processions ever held – for Richard II and Charles II – had much in common. Both Kings rode through the streets to the sounds of trumpets and other musical instruments, accompanied by nobles, knights, the Commons and aldermen. Charles's progress, though, was especially slow as he stopped to enjoy the shows – with topical themes such as the return of the monarch and the rout of rebellion – provided for his entertainment. The crowds in their turn enjoyed the King's hospitality – as indeed they would all next day – in the form of the wine flowing from the conduit in Cheapside.

THE CORONATION CEREMONY AND THE CROWN JEWELS

The dress of the two Kings gives the first clue as to the essential difference between the two occasions. The young Richard rode through the streets bare-headed, dressed all in white, as were many of those accompanying him, to symbolize his suitability for consecration. His appearance bore witness to the solemnity of the ritual he was to undergo the following day. By 1661 the philosophy of the Tudors and Stuarts prevailed: kings were God's anointed 'not in respect of the oil the bishop useth, but in consideration of their power . . . The oil, if added, is but a ceremony; if it be wanting, that king is yet a perfect monarch notwithstanding, and God's anointed, as well as if he was inoiled.' Charles cut a splendid figure in a high-crowned hat liberally adorned with feathers and a richly embroidered suit of purple velvet trimmed with ermine. Even his stirrups were set with some of the 320 precious stones used for his accoutrements. His horse was caparisoned with cloth-of-gold and fur.

The coronation of Charles II was the last to include the traditional riding procession (Vigil Procession). The Lord Mayor and aldermen of the City of London put on a magnificent show to mark the end of the 'dismal Night of Usurpation and Oppression'. The diarist John Evelyn was impressed by the large triumphal arches erected along the route, their 'good invention and architecture, with inscriptions'. From their vantage point at 'Mr Young's the Flagg-maker in Cornhill', Samuel Pepys and his wife admired the costumes of the riders; 'imbroidery and diamonds were ordinary among them'.

THE CORONATION CEREMONY AND THE CROWN JEWELS

After taking dinner with his closest supporters the medieval king was then expected to spend the night in prayer and contemplation, attended by the Abbot, or another cleric designated by him, who acted as his spiritual mentor. (This spiritual cleansing was not deemed necessary for the eleven-year-old Richard, probably because of his age, but even so he spent the evening quietly, retiring early after being ritually bathed.)

Henry IV, Richard II's usurper, made a confession on the morning of his coronation in 1399 and also heard Mass three times. The day before he had created a number of new knights by a ritual which involved a bath. The institution of this pseudo-Order was politically rather than spiritually inspired, however, with Henry using it as a way of increasing the number of his sworn supporters. Thereafter it became the custom for every new king to create Knights of the Bath on the day before his coronation. The tradition died out after the coronation of Charles II.

The lower status of a queen-consort in relation to her husband was reflected in the coronation orders drawn up at Canterbury between the tenth and twelfth centuries. She received only a crown and ring and, in theory, her crowning and consecration could be performed by a priest as well as a bishop, whereas a king could only be crowned by a bishop. There is no record, however, of a priest ever performing the ritual.

The monks of Westminster's belief that their devising of richer ceremonials would increase the prestige of the Abbey and St Edward's regalia led to greater elaboration of the coronation rituals for queen-consorts. The coronation prescription for queen-consorts given in the Little Device, compiled in English for the coronation of Richard III and his Queen, Anne Neville, in 1483, calls for the delivery of a sceptre and rod in addition to the usual crown and ring.

Since the late Middle Ages it has been normal for a queen-consort to be crowned with her husband, although his ceremonials take precedence over hers. William the Conqueror was most reluctant to be crowned without his wife, Mathilda. Expediency forced his hand, but William ensured that when she did eventually join him in England a second

This illustration, taken from the late fourteenth-century Liber Regalis *or 'Royal Book' devised at Westminster, depicts a king and queen seated in full royal state on their thrones at coronation. It was customary for the queen to be seated on the left side of her husband. After her coronation the queen would make a slight obeisance to the king before mounting the scaffold to take her place beside him. A Te Deum was sung as the king ascended to his throne but was not repeated for the queen. The union of the king and queen was signalled by the Abbot of Westminster when he administered wine to them from the same chalice after Communion. The* Liber Regalis *came to be regarded as an invaluable source of coronation ritual and was eventually kept with the regalia itself.*

Elizabeth of York, the Queen of Henry VII, was one of the few consorts to be complimented with an independent coronation. The pageantry which attended her crowning was devised by Henry down to details such as her dress and the preparation of her litter.

crowning was performed. Not all queen-consorts have been crowned. Henrietta Maria, the Catholic queen of Charles I, was not crowned. Of Henry VIII's six wives only the first two were crowned. Catherine of Aragon was Henry's wife at the time of his accession and so was crowned with him. Anne Boleyn received the compliment of an independent coronation.

Controversy surrounded Henry's marriage to Anne, as it had Edward IV's to Elizabeth Woodville. Edward's secret marriage to Elizabeth greatly displeased some of his Yorkist supporters, including the most powerful nobleman in the land, Richard Neville, Earl of Warwick, who had intended that the king should marry a foreign princess. Both Kings responded to their critics by purposely devising splendid independent coronations for their Queens. Henry VII heralded his successful uniting of the formerly warring houses of York and Lancaster by giving his new bride – Elizabeth of York, the daughter of Edward IV – a lavish coronation of her own.

ELIZABETHA · VXOR
HENRICI · VII ·

The water pageantry that would become such a feature of later Tudor coronations first appeared at Elizabeth's coronation in 1487. The ceremonials began the day before the queen's Vigil Procession. Elizabeth was first met on the Thames on her journey up from Greenwich to the Tower by the mayor, sheriffs and aldermen of London, and by members of the craft guilds in barges decorated with silver banners and streamers. One barge called the Bachelor's Barge carried a large red dragon which spouted fire, an allusion to the Tudors' Welsh origins. From other craft musicians played and symbolic devices were presented for the queen's pleasure. This reception of the Queen two days before her coronation would become a standard ceremony for some fifty years. The pagaentry of such civic receptions was, however, or became less spontaneous

THE CORONATION CEREMONY AND THE CROWN JEWELS

than it may have appeared on the surface, with kings – notably Henry VII – taking a hand in choreographing the proceedings.

The Little Device was the last set of orders devised by the monks of Westminster. In 1538 Henry VIII's campaign against the monasteries and the alleged superstitious worship of saints brought the destruction of the shrine of St Edward in the Abbey and the transfer to the king's treasury of the gold, silver and jewels which had accrued there since the reign of Henry III. Two years later the monastery was dissolved and transformed into the cathedral of a diocese of Westminster.

The implications for the coronation ceremony of Henry's rift with the Church of Rome and his assumption of the headship of the Church of England did not become apparent until the accession of Edward VI in 1547. The ceremony devised for Edward's coronation was shaped by the strongly Protestant Lord Protector Somerset, the most powerful man in England during the years of the king's minority, and the Archbishop of Canterbury, Thomas Cranmer.

The most radical aspect of the ceremony was the considerably reduced role of churchmen, traditionally the intermediaries between God and the king. This was due to the playing down of the role of St Edward's regalia as holy relics. The ceremonials of divesting and returning the regalia to St Edward's altar and, in particular, of delivering St Edward's Crown and receiving a new one disappeared. The part played by the Archbishop in the delivery of the regalia, other than the crowns, was abolished, although he may have delivered St Edward's Staff. The task of divesting the King of his clothes in readiness for anointing now fell to the Lord Great Chamberlain. Only two ceremonial tasks were assigned to the Bishop or Dean of Westminster – drying the anointed places with a cotton or linen cloth and deliver-

The remodelling of Westminster Abbey included extending the east end into a long apsed chapel, known as St Edward's Chapel, at the end of which was set a shrine to the Confessor. Over some 30 years Henry III collected precious stones, cameos, gold and silver to decorate the shrine. St Edward's remains were transferred to this site on its completion in 1265.

ing the royal buskins (soft boots reaching to just below the knees) and spurs to the Lord Great Chamberlain. St Edward's regalia were used including, most importantly, St Edward's Crown, but the King was not dressed in the vestments of St Edward, probably because of his small size.

This secularization of parts of the coronation ritual deeply disturbed his successor, Mary I. The queen was appalled by the fact that she could do nothing to alter the form of the ritual until after her coronation — because only as the crowned head could she call Parliament and have them repeal Edward's 'blasphemous and impious laws' — and requested of the Church of Rome absolution for herself and Archbishop Gardiner of Winchester, who was to crown her.

Under Elizabeth I the process began of purging the Church of all alleged superstitious beliefs and practices and transforming it into a true Church of England. At her coronation both the Epistle and Gospel were first sung in Latin and then read in English. Elizabeth was determined on eradicating from the services of the Church aspects that she did not believe in. The delivery of the ornaments were restored to a bishop but, like her half-brother, she was not vested in St Edward's robes; James I would be the first monarch to revert to this practice. Most significantly

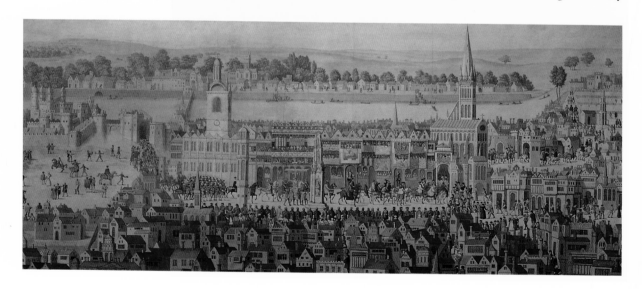

of all, although Mass was celebrated, it is thought that the Queen retired into a closet beside the altar when the Host was raised, thus signalling her disapproval of the Catholic doctrine of transubstantiation. When the dust from the Civil War had well and truly settled, after the 'Glorious Revolution' of 1688 brought William and Mary to the throne, a declaration repudiating this doctrine would be inserted in the coronation service.

Elizabeth I was quick to reverse the retreat from Anglicanism begun by her Roman Catholic sister, Mary I. Her intention of ridding the services of the Church of all practices and beliefs she deemed superstitious was first signalled at Christmas 1558, before her coronation, when during Mass she withdrew from her chapel at the elevation of the Host. The title of Supreme Head of the Church of England which Henry VIII had declared himself and his successors to be in 1534 was denied her, however. She was called the 'Supreme Governor', a distinction which meant nothing in practice but satisfied the consciences of those who objected to the headship altogether and those who would not confer it on a woman. Under Elizabeth the Prayer Book of 1552 was restored, with a few modifications, as the only lawful lituirgy.

THE CORONATION CEREMONY AND THE CROWN JEWELS

William of Orange, the nephew and son-in-law of James II, led an armed force to England in defence of Protestantism after entering into a secret alliance with leading Whig and Tory politicians. Three months after landing at Torbay on 5 November 1688, William and his wife, Mary, were offered the crown jointly. The offer was conditional on them accepting a new Bill of Rights safeguarding the constitution and securing the Protestant succession. This defining of the monarch's power in relation to Parliament was reflected in the order for the coronation ceremony.

All coronations since the accession of William and Mary have been based on the revisions devised for their joint ceremony by Henry Compton, the Bishop of London. The Communion was reinstated – it had been dropped for the coronation of James II – but divided into two: the first part coming after the Litany and before the declaration and oath, the second after the homage. An Act of Parliament of 1689 ensured that all future monarchs would have to promise to uphold Protestantism as the one true religion of the nation.

The direction of the secular parts of the coronation ceremony became the office of a great nobleman in the late fifteenth century. That someone should undertake this task was made necessary by the late medieval elaboration of the ceremony and its attendant processions, and from the coronation of Richard III in 1483 the responsibility was assigned to the Lord Great Chamberlain. Another royal officer, the Earl Marshal, became responsible for the ordering of the main processions.

THE CORONATION CEREMONY AND THE CROWN JEWELS

Fees — usually in kind — were given for performing many of the tasks. The Lord Great Chamberlain at Queen Anne's coronation, for example, had a right to receive, among other things, furniture and tapestry used by the queen on the eve of her coronation. The Royal Almoner, who was responsible for distributing the leavings from the feast to the poor, received a large silver dish from the royal table and also laid claim to a tun of wine (252 old gallons). Traditional perquisites of this kind were drastically reduced and, in some cases, abolished altogether after the costly coronation of George IV in 1821.

Conversely, the right of performing some services was given to those willing to pay for the honour. At Richard I's second coronation the payment of two hundred marks secured for the citizens of London the right of serving drink to the King.

The giving of perks did not always assist the smooth-running of the event. At the second coronation of King Stephen in the twelfth century the anthem 'Christus vincit' was allegedly ruined because the clergy tried to outsing the monks and beat them to the end of it and to the customary fee from the King. The clergy were excommunicated by Archbishop Theobald while the monks received the praise of Stephen and Mathilda.

At the coronation of Charles II the Barons of the Cinque Ports had to defend their traditional perk — the canopy which they had held over the King during the opening and closing processions — against the predatory designs of the King's footmen. The Barons, it seems, were dragged bodily down Westminster Hall as they clung to their canopy. The footmen eventually gave up and later, when the King heard the tale, were arrested, imprisoned and dismissed.

Until this century brought a change in attitudes, practising any part of the ceremonial was thought beneath the monarch's dignity. Before the Abbot of Westminster was established in the role of guiding the king through the ritual on the day of coronation, it is thought that the task must have been performed by some cleric. Indeed few monarchs have understood the ceremonial sufficiently to go through their coronation

A. The *QUEENS* Majestie.
B. The Bishop of London.
C. The Bishop of Winchester.
D. The Dutchess of Norfolk.
E. Four Earls Daughters.

F. Sixteen Barons of the Cinque ports.
G. a Lady of the Bed chamber.
H. Two of her Maties women.
I. Gentlemen Pensioners.

THE CORONATION CEREMONY AND THE CROWN JEWELS

70

unprompted. Queen Victoria attended one short rehearsal before her coronation and, it is said, 'never knew what to do next' on the day itself. Only the Archbishop of Canterbury and Lord Thynne, acting for the Dean of Westminster, had rehearsed their parts. At one point the Bishop of Bath and Wells told the Queen that the service was finished and allowed her to process to St Edward's Chapel before he realized that he had in fact turned two pages at once and that she would have to return to the throne to complete the ceremony.

Elizabeth II's coronation was, by comparison, free of such organizational hiccups. The Queen and her attendants even went so far as to practice their roles at Buckingham Palace, using white sheets pinned together to serve as her train.

The coronation procession of James II and Mary of Modena in 1685. The carrying of the canopy over the royal head was one of the many eagerly sought after services performed at coronation. The Cinque Ports – originally a federation of the ports of Hastings, Romney, Hythe, Dover and Sandwich – were granted this particular privilege in the Middle Ages in recognition of their important function as providers of ships for the sovereign. For the duration of the ceremony the representatives of the ports were granted the title baron. They were also rewarded by the gift of the canopy they bore in the procession.

THE CORONATION CEREMONY AND THE CROWN JEWELS

'THE PARK PRESENTED A CURIOUS SPECTACLE, crowds of people up to Constitution Hill, soldiers, bands etc . . . At half-past nine I went into the next room, dressed exactly in my House of Lords costume . . . At ten I got into the State Coach . . . and we began our Progress. It was a fine day, and the crowds of people exceeded what I have ever seen . . . Their good-humour and excessive loyalty was beyond everything, and I really cannot say how proud I feel to be the Queen of such a Nation.'

Queen Victoria was only the second monarch in the long history of the coronation to begin her great day processing by carriage from Buckingham Palace to the Abbey. This colourful opening flourish had been introduced for the coronation of Victoria's uncle, William IV, in 1831 and was a partial revival of the old cavalcade through the City of London on the eve of coronation, called the Vigil Procession. It replaced the opening walking procession from Westminster Palace to the Abbey which had been a feature of coronations since the early Middle Ages.

Preceding spread: Queen Elizabeth II leaving Buckingham Palace in the state coach for her coronation at Westminster Abbey in 1953. Buckingham Palace has been the main royal residence since the reign of Queen Victoria, who soon came to love the place despite its initial drawbacks of faulty drains, bells and windows. George IV conceived the idea for a palace fit for a king of England while he was regent. Work began on the project shortly after his accession, but he did not live to see the house completed.

The Great Hall was built by William Rufus in 1099 as part of his plan to enlarge the Confessor's Palace of Westminster. Until 1327 it was used as the coronation banqueting hall. Thereafter, it also became the scene of the formal preliminaries to coronation, of electing the king and lifting him onto a raised seat, activities which had previously taken place in the original hall of the Palace, known as the Lesser Hall. The oak hammer-beamed roof was among the several alterations made to the Hall by Richard II in the late fourteenth century.

Westminster Palace served as the main royal residence and home of the court until 1512, when Henry VIII moved to Whitehall Palace. Its role as the administrative centre of the kingdom was not affected by this move, however.

Much of the pageantry which had grown up around the walking procession was transferred to the new procession, which would eventually comprise several separate cavalcades, such as the Lord Mayor's procession from Mansion House, probably one of the most famous of them all.

The formal election by a council of lords and prelates which early English kings had to undergo as an indispensable preliminary to coronation took place on the morning of the ceremony. For kings who were to be crowned in Westminster Abbey, Westminster Hall became the traditional place of election. (The original Hall, now known as the Lesser Hall of the Palace, was used until 1327. Thereafter the Great Hall, built by William Rufus in 1099, became the setting for this ceremony.) After the formal election, which ended with the king being lifted onto a raised seat (or throne), the king was taken in procession to his coronation.

The Opening Procession

The form, style and composition of this opening procession to the coronation church changed significantly over the centuries. At the coronation of King Edgar, for example, in 973, the procession was made up of clergy and chief abbots, followed by the abbesses and their nuns.

THE CORONATION CEREMONY AND THE CROWN JEWELS

Women religious would not be accorded the same high status after the end of the Anglo-Saxon age. Edgar's coronation provides the first historical record of what was almost certainly already established practice, the leading of the king into the church by two bishops. From at least as early as Richard I's coronation in 1189, it became customary for the Bishops of Durham and Bath and Wells to support the monarch in this way. This tradition suffered temporary interruption during the Reformation; Edward VI was supported by a bishop and an earl, the latter taking precedence by walking on the King's right.

The composition of the opening procession was restricted to clerics and nobles until the reign of Henry VIII. At the coronation of his second wife, Anne Boleyn, Henry's desire to broaden the base of his support was reflected in the admittance of the mayor and aldermen of London to the procession; at previous coronations their participation had been confined to the coronation feast after the ceremony and, of course, witnessing the ceremony in the Abbey.

The order for the coronation of Edward III in 1327 called for the king to adopt an attitude of humility as he processed to the Abbey, bare-headed, dressed in white and wearing only buskins on his feet. The coronation of Henry IV in 1399 marked a change in the style of dress, the king appearing in a red gown, a long red mantle and a fur-trimmed chaperon; the last-mentioned a type of hood which was often worn twisted into a kind of turban. In this period it was traditional for the king to issue through the Great Wardrobe special scarlet or red robes and liveries to many of the officers in his household.

Rich red parliamentary robes and a cap of estate, or maintenance, would become the usual attire for monarchs on their way to coronation. Originally a type of royal and princely headgear of honour worn by the king and used for the investiture of dukes, the cap came to be worn by marquesses in the fifteenth century, by earls in the sixteenth century, under Edward VI, and viscounts in the seventeenth century, under James I. The robes are first mentioned at the coronation of Anne Boleyn in 1533. There have been a few departures from the custom of wearing royal

The simplicity which characterized early medieval coronations had been lost by the end of the fifteenth century. No longer humble supplicants, kings now processed to their coronations in sumptuous attire appropriate to their royal status. Echoes of the splendour of Henry VIII's coronation procession are captured in this depiction of Henry processing to Parliament in 1512. The king's robe of crimson velvet trimmed with ermine is similar to the one he wore three years earlier, as is the collar or chain of jewels around his neck.

red (properly crimson). Mary of Modena wore purple velvet at her coronation with James II in 1685 – provoking mutterings in Puritan quarters because of the colour's Papist connotations – as did Wilhelmina Caroline some forty years later, although quite uncontroversially by this time. Unusually, William III wore a hoop of gold over his cap of estate, probably to signify that he came to his coronation as elected governor (Stadholder) of Holland. The Hanoverian kings, all the Georges and William IV, would follow William's precedent. Peers traditionally carry their coronets in the opening procession; at the coronation of Charles II the grandest of the peers had their coronets carried for them.

Throughout the Middle Ages the privilege of bearing the swords, sceptres and crown in the opening procession was regarded as the right of

THE CORONATION CEREMONY AND THE CROWN JEWELS

the senior earls, with perhaps preference given to those related to the king. The honour of bearing St Edward's regalia was granted to the magnates by Edward II on the morning of his coronation in 1308. Edward's decision was greeted with alarm by the monks of Westminster, who considered that they alone had the right to handle these holy relics and that the magnates should confine themselves to carrying the king's personal regalia. Edward, however, had been in no position to argue and in addition to acceding to the magnates' demands in this respect had also been forced to promise a second banishment for his recently returned favourite, Piers Gaveston, after the coronation. The hostility of the magnates to Gaveston, especially of the king's cousin Thomas of Lancaster, had been exacerbated by his recent elevation to the rank of senior earl, giving him the right to bear St Edward's Crown in the

In front of Henry is Edward, Duke of Buckingham, holding the royal cap of maintenance; and behind, the Earl of Oxford, bearing the staff of the Lord Great Chamberlain. In 1509 seven men wearing surcoats of arms denoting the sources of Henry's inheritance of his office processed behind the King. Heraldic imagery is in evidence here too, in the Tudor rose on the roof of the canopy, the man in the surcoat of royal devices and the heraldic banners at the rear.

THE CORONATION CEREMONY AND THE CROWN JEWELS

Afhaaling van de Koninglyke Cieraaden uit den Tour.

Top: *The regalia being brought from the Tower to Westminster Hall in readiness for the coronation of William and Mary in 1689. By this date custody of the regalia was the sole responsibility of the Master of the Jewel House at the Tower.*

Below: *Part of the coronation procession of James II in 1685. The King is depicted wearing Parliamentary robes – the train held by four sons of peers – and his fur-trimmed cap of estate. On either side of him are his traditional 'supporters', the bishops of Durham and Bath and Wells. The regalia is borne before him. The peers hold their coronets in their hands. The cloth-of-gold canopy, to each corner of which is attached a silver-gilt bell, is held over the King by sixteen barons of the Cinque Ports.*

opening procession. The additional honour of redeeming and bearing the Sword of Offering was also assigned to Gaveston. Thomas was given the distinction of bearing the sword Curtana.

Later in the fourteenth century the procedure would become established of the Abbot of Westminster sending St Edward's regalia to the Palace on the eve of coronation in readiness for the procession. The Sword of State and the other swords together with the spurs borne in the opening procession were never part of St Edward's regalia and so were not among the insignia traditionally brought to the Hall and surrendered to the king's officers. At the coronation of Charles II they were delivered by the Master of the Jewel House to the Lord High Constable at Westminster

Hall and laid out on a table with the other items of regalia. The noblemen deputed to bear the ornaments were then summoned to the table by Garter Principal at Arms.

The distribution of the regalia in the Hall was accomplished with almost theatrical flair at the coronation of Charles I. The King's favourite, George Villiers, delivered each item to his sovereign on bended knee for Charles to then hand individually to the noblemen and bishops chosen to bear them. Items of personal regalia, which did not figure in the opening procession but were required for the ceremony or the closing procession, such as the Imperial State Crown, other sceptres and bracelets, were taken straight to the Abbey for the king's final change.

For the coronation of Edward I in 1274 a timber walkway was erected from the doorway of the Lesser Hall, the scene of the King's formal election by clergy and nobles, to the Abbey. It became customary to lay blue cloth along the whole length of the processional route, ending at the altar. Some 2,114 yards in all were used for this purpose at George I's coronation. Blue is still the traditional colour of the coronation carpet laid along the nave of the Abbey.

For many centuries it was customary to strew the processional route with herbs and flowers. A few hours before the procession for the coronation of James II in 1685 'nine baskets full of sweete herbs and flowers' were scattered by Mary Dowle, 'Strewer of Herbs in Ordinary to his Majesty', and six assistants.

The walkway was canopied for the first time for the coronation of Edward II in 1308, and at all subsequent coronations which featured a walking procession. On the occasion of Edward's coronation the crush of onlookers was so great that the procession could barely make its way to the Abbey. Edward entered the Abbey by a back route to avoid the indignity of fighting his way through the crowd. This scrum was repeated inside the Abbey itself, with the King and the three

officiating bishops pressed on from all sides during the ceremony. A strong wall behind the altar gave way under the pressure, killing one man.

Improvements to the organization of coronations greatly reduced the scope for incidents of this kind. It would seem, however, if the story of William III having his purse stolen on the way to his coronation of 1689 is true, that the opening procession would continue to bring the monarch into close contact with 'baser personages' for several centuries more. By the time of the coronation of George II guards were posted along the processional route. The walkway was raised some eighteen inches off the ground for this coronation.

The abandonment of the opening walking procession after the coronation of George IV in 1821 necessitated re-organizing the procession of clerics and choristers, which now took place within the Abbey. The items of regalia were collected from St Edward's Chapel and then taken to an annexe erected outside the west door of the Abbey, where the monarch and those who would accompany him down the nave to the altar waited. After the distribution of the regalia to those designated to bear it, the monarch's procession sets off.

 First Sightings Inside the Abbey

The organization of the event within the Abbey improved with the provision of seating. Special enclosures and stands were earmarked for the exclusive use of the good and the great, such as nobles, ambassadors, heralds, privy councillors, aldermen, judges and other gentlemen. Additional scaffolds were also provided for 'Persons of all Conditions to sit'. It was to one of these that Samuel Pepys made his way in 1661, 'with much ado', having risen at four o'clock after a night of enthusiastic revellry in anticipation of the great day. Pepys found himself in almost exclusively male company for the coronation of Charles II. As the main procession was not due to arrive in the Abbey until eleven o'clock, and he was denied the opportunity of indulging his favourite hobby of eyeing pretty women, the hours must have seemed especially long.

Queen Elizabeth and the Duke of Edinburgh arriving at the annexe at the West Door of Westminster Abbey. The Queen is wearing an ivory gown, designed by Norman Hartnell, embroidered with patriotic motifs, Parliamentary robes flowing in customary style down her back and the diamond circlet of George IV. The ornament has four sprays, each of them composed of a rose, thistle and shamrock, patriotic motifs of the United Kingdom; the same motifs can be seen on the splendid Sword of Offering also made for King George's coronation. The Duke, here wearing the uniform of an Admiral of the Fleet, will change into his Parliament robes inside the annexe.

A foreign observer attending the coronation of William and Mary in 1689 was amazed by the extent of the seating. The stands reached 'quite to the House Tops' and 'fill'd up the Spaces on each Side all the Way'. Some space in the Abbey, and also along the processional route, was let out to private contractors to help offset some of the costs of coronation. At George III's coronation front seats in the galleries overlooking the 'theatre' — the raised area in front of the altar where the key parts of the ceremony take place — cost ten guineas each.

The issuing of personal invitations has not prevented the occasional altercation over the seating arrangements in the Abbey. The Venetian and Sicilian ambassadors attending the coronation of George II in 1727 fell to squabbling over their places. In the Middle Ages all important people in the realm were invited to attend the king's coronation. From the first, these included bishops, abbots and noblemen. Later, representatives from the larger towns were invited also.

The American-born MP Sir Henry ('Chips') Channon and his wife were among the 7,700 people invited to attend the coronation of George VI in 1937. In his memoirs Channon writes of arriving at the Abbey around half past eight in the morning and from their places in the south transept, immediately behind the viscounts and barons, watching the processions of dignitaries, culminating in the arrival of the main procession: the foreign royals and their entourage, among them the 'gaunt Queen of Norway', the 'tiny English princesses excited by their coronets and trains', the Duchesses of Kent and Gloucester 'looking staggering', and Queen Mary 'ablaze, regal and over-powering'. From his vantage point at the north end of the Abbey, Pepys glimpsed the red-carpeted 'theatre' and 'all the officers of all kinds, so much as the very fidlers, in red vests', but, unlike the Channons, he could not see the King invested.

Keeping body and soul together was not the problem in 1661 that it would become for congregations at later coronations. Pepys could fortify himself with fruit, wine, sandwiches and other provisions sold by confectioners at the back of one of the galleries. These arrangements ceased after the coronation of Queen Victoria in 1838. At subsequent coronations forward planning at an individual level was required if hunger pangs were to be staved off during the five hours of ceremonials in the Abbey. The young Duchess of Marlborough was one of the peeresses attending Edward VII's coronation who hid chocolate in her pocket for covert consumption.

 ## The Overture

Both Charles II in 1661 and Elizabeth II in 1953 entered the Abbey to the strains of Psalm 122 ('I was glad when they said to me, Let us go into the house of the Lord'). Charles stopped about a third of the way up the nave and made his private devotion, while most of the members of the procession took their seats. Elizabeth proceeded directly to the 'theatre', her regalia borne before her.

George IV's coronation procession was by all accounts a magnificent sight, mainly because of the unusual costumes which the King himself had devised for the ceremony. The King's officers and Privy Councillors had initially reacted with alarm at the prospect of being clad in blue and

George IV applied his enthusiasm for devising uniforms to the task of designing the costumes for his coronation in 1821. Naturally, the apparel he designed for himself was the pièce de résistance. The King is depicted here with his eight train-bearers, all the eldest sons of earls, and the Master of the Robes (far right); the latter was responsible for commissioning the royal robes, caps and vestments.

THE CORONATION CEREMONY AND THE CROWN JEWELS

THE CORONATION CEREMONY AND THE CROWN JEWELS

gold satin doublets, trunk hose and cloaks. In the event they cut quite a dash, their attire one of the most striking features of the ceremony.

The King was dressed in cloth-of-silver lavishly trimmed with gold lace and braid, silver ribbon garters adorned with gold lace rosettes and white kid shoes with red heels and gold lace rosettes. His headgear was equally remarkable: a large hat with upturned brim, diamond loop, a heron's feather aigrette in brilliants and a diamond circlet, all of which was worn over a long curly wig. According to one observer, at the King's entrance the whole assembly rose 'with a sort of feathered silken thunder. Plumes wave, eyes sparkle, glasses are out, mouths smile' and the man who has become the object of their attention 'shows like some gorgeous bird of the East'.

The cost of the ceremonial dress made for George's coronation exceeded the total expenditure of £42,298 for William IV's coronation. Estimates of the cost of George's coronation range from between £238,000, the official figure, and more than £400,000; £100,000 of the total was voted by Parliament with the balance of the official figure met by indemnities from France as a consequence of her defeat in the Napoleonic Wars.

Not surprisingly, given the heat of the day and his sixty years, George reportedly looked strained by the exertion of bearing the weight of his robes. Queen Wilhelmina Caroline, George II's wife, remarked the day after her coronation in 1727 that 'what had fatigued her most was the weight of her skirt'. According to Lord Hervey, 'The dress of the Queen [which reputedly cost £6,000] on this occasion was as fine as the accumulated riches of the City and suburbs could make it; for besides her own jewels (which were a great number and very valuable) she had on her head and on her shoulders all the pearls she could borrow of the ladies of quality . . ., and on her petticoat, all the diamonds she could hire'. The London jewellers, it was reported, did not have gems enough for her costume and were forced to send to Paris and Holland for more.

The number and sex of the train-bearers has varied. Wilhelmina Caroline's train was carried by her three eldest daughters, assisted by four

Queen Elizabeth making her way down the nave towards the altar, accompanied by her traditional 'supporters', six train-bearers and, bringing up the rear, the Mistress of the Robes. Few of the thousands of guests invited to attend a coronation are fortunate enough to get a clear view of the main parts of the ceremony. Printed service books help them to keep abreast of proceedings. Many of the guests are seated in temporary galleries erected for the occasion. For the coronation of George V in 1911, 200 men of the Brigade of Guards were used to test the stability of these galleries.

THE CORONATION CEREMONY AND THE CROWN JEWELS

ladies. In 1902, Queen Alexandra chose six boys instead of girls. The Queen and her ladies experienced the utmost difficulty in making any progress through the new deep pile blue carpet laid especially for this and subsequent coronations. Some of the elderly peers attending the coronation of George VI about thirty years later would be similarly impeded. Elizabeth II, aware of these past problems, ensured that a shallow pile carpet was laid for her coronation in 1953. Despite this sensible alteration, Elizabeth found herself becalmed at one point in the ceremony when the carpet held the metal fringe of the brocaded gold mantle she was wearing.

The Acclamation

When the procession up the nave reaches the presbytery the monarch is saluted by a chanted acclamation. The precedent for this was set at the coronation of James II and Mary of Modena in 1685, with 'Vivat Jacobus Rex'. The monarch mounts the steps of the 'theatre' and proceeds to the chair of state facing the altar. At the coronation of Queen Anne three footstalls were strategically placed to help alleviate the painful effects of the chronic gout from which she was thought to suffer. (This affliction had also caused the Queen to be chaired along the processional route.) At the coronation of James and Mary the King went to a platform on the south side of the 'theatre', the Queen to a lower one on the north side.

In the very earliest coronation orders the king's first action on reaching the altar was to prostrate himself before it. While he did this, the Te Deum was sung. The king was then lifted up for presentation to the congregation, who had to give their assent to the earlier formal election by nobles and clerics in Westminster Hall. This assent was similar in form to the acclamation given to a Roman emperor on election. The tumultuous acclamation that greeted William the Conqueror so terrified his Norman guards that, according to one eye-witness, William of Poitiers, they believed the congregation to be on the point of rebellion.

From the early thirteenth century onwards, perhaps even earlier, a scaffold was erected so that the king could show himself to the

Queen Elizabeth entering the area where the main coronation ceremonials take place. Part of the raised area, or 'theatre', is visible on the right of the photograph. The seniority of the Bishop of Durham over the Bishop of Bath and Wells is indicated by his position on the sovereign's right. Their right to the privilege of 'supporting' the sovereign during the ceremony dates to the coronation of Richard I in 1189.

The scaffold or raised area on which the king stood to show himself to the congregation was from the coronation of Henry IV in 1399 (depicted here) laid with coverings and hung round with cloth-of-gold and silk. The order for the ceremony also stipulated that the throne – set high so that the King could be clearly seen by all – should be entirely covered with silk, set with cushions and have steps leading up to it from the west side and steps down from it on the east side. Archbishop Cranmer's account of the coronation of Edward VI in 1547 mentions that the scaffold had 22 steps leading up to it on the side of the choir and 15 on the side of the high altar. A plinth of seven steps supported the throne.

congregation at the acclamation, after crowning and for the enthronement. The platform erected for the coronation of Edward II in 1308 was supported by wooden piers and high enough off the ground to allow barons, knights and other nobles to ride underneath it. The 'theatre' for the coronation of Elizabeth II in 1953 was raised only a few feet.

The coronation of Henry VI in 1429 provides the clearest existing record of the form of the assent in late medieval times. Henry was presented by the Archbishop at the four corners of the scaffold erected at the crossing in the Abbey, between the choir in the nave and the high altar: first to the people on the north and south of the scaffold and then to the lords on the east and the clergy on the west of the choir. The Archbishop introduced the King with the following words: 'Sirs, here cometh Harry, King Harry the fifth's son, humbly to God and Holy Church, asking the crown of this realm by right and descent of heritage. If ye hold you well pleased withal and will be pleased with him, say you now "yea" and hold up your hands.' Those present then cried in unison 'yea', 'yea'.

The acclamation marked the culmination of the process of election begun in Westminster Hall and one of the most significant lay elements of

THE CORONATION CEREMONY AND THE CROWN JEWELS

coronation. A right to the throne based on primogeniture replaced election as the principle of succession after the reign of King John (1199–1216). However, election still remained as a theoretical right and continued to exist in coronation as a formal confirmation in the Palace and as an acclamation in the Abbey. Amendments to the form of the Archbishop's request to the congregation would reflect the fact that monarchs now went to their coronation as monarchs and not as monarchs-elect. In 1483 the Archbishop of Canterbury showed Richard III to the people with the words: 'Sirs here is present Richard rightful and undoubted inheritor by the laws of God and man to the crown and royal dignity of England with all things thereunto annexed and appertaining, elected chosen and required by all the three estates [nobility, clergy and commoners] of this same land to take upon him the said crown and royal dignity . . . Will ye sirs at this time give your willingness and assent to [his] consecration, anointing and coronation.' The assent to coronation was thus changed to recognition of a king's established right.

One of the most important changes to the wording of the recognition in recent history was necessitated by Britain's relinquishment of most of her empire in 1931. When George VI came to the throne some five years later he was styled 'His Most Excellent Majesty George VI, of Great Britain, Ireland and of the British Dominions beyond the Seas, King, Defender of the Faith, Emperor of India' but no formula acceptable to all the self-governing nations of the new Commonwealth could be agreed upon for the recognition. George was, therefore, simply presented as 'King George, your undoubted King'.

A first oblation of an altar cloth, called a pall, and a gold brick weighing 1lb used to be offered by the monarch after the acclamation. In the modern ceremony one oblation is made, after Communion.

 The Oath

Consistent with the medieval emphasis on coronation as confirmation of a right conferred by men and God was the notion that the people's assent was dependent on the king's undertaking to defend and preserve the

THE CORONATION CEREMONY AND THE CROWN JEWELS

Church and his people and to rule justly. This promise (*promissio regis*), later called the coronation oath, has been part of English coronation since orders for the conduct of the ritual were first formulated in the late ninth century. At this time, however, the promise came at the end of the service, after prayers, a blessing and enthronement. Thereafter until the thirteenth century the oath preceded the people's assent.

The form of the oath was probably influenced by Byzantine practice. The Byzantine emperors had since the late eighth century taken an oath, written and spoken, which, although essentially a profession of orthodoxy, also contained a commitment to benevolent and just rule. The king's promise instituted by the Anglo-Saxons contained three undertakings: to keep the Church and all Christian people in peace; to forbid robbery and all wrong-doing in men of all rank; and to exercise justice and mercy in all judgements. Although variations would occur as a result of the differing priorities of individual kings, these three undertakings remained the basis of the oath and still do to this day; Richard II, for example, added an undertaking to the effect that he would improve upon his predecessors' record of protecting and advancing the work of the Church.

From the accession of Henry I (1100) there may also have been a tendency to include in the oath an undertaking to abolish bad new laws and maintain good old ones popularly associated with Edward the Confessor and other Anglo-Saxon kings. At his coronation Henry emulated his Anglo-Saxon predecessors, either Edward or Ethelred, by placing a copy of the oath on the high altar to signify his good faith.

The oath taken by Edward II contained a new clause pledging him to accept in future the laws chosen by the 'community of the realm', a stipulation introduced as a result of his father's attempt to side-step disagreeable obligations. In 1305 Edward I had given great offence by obtaining a bull from Pope Clement V absolving him from the undertakings that he had been forced to agree to by his barons. In the new form the Archbishop recited the oath and to each clause the King had to respond with 'I promise' or some equivalent.

Seated on the chair of state facing the high altar the sovereign listens as the Archbishop of Canterbury asks her the traditional 'several Questions' as a preliminary to administering the Oath. The Queen swears 'to govern the peoples of the United Kingdom of Great Britain and Northern Ireland'. After the Oath has been taken, the sovereign is led to the coronation chair.

THE CORONATION CEREMONY AND THE CROWN JEWELS

THE CORONATION CEREMONY AND THE CROWN JEWELS

The form of the oath did not change greatly until the coronation of William and Mary in 1689. The wording of the oath now reflected the altered status of the monarch in relation to Parliament. The sovereign had to promise to govern 'according to the Statutes in Parliament agreed on'. The English Church, which since the ninth century monarchs had promised to uphold, was now clearly defined as the 'Protestant reformed religion established by law'. A declaration repudiating the doctrine of transubstantiation and other Catholic tenets was inserted before the oath for the coronation of Queen Anne. After 1761 this declaration was made before Parliament. The Accession Declaration Act of 1910 watered down its content to a simple promise to be 'a faithful Protestant'.

From the fourteenth century until the Commonwealth the usual form of swearing the oath was on the consecrated Host and the Gospels. Edward VI and his half-sister, Mary Tudor, took the oath on the Sacrament but not, it seems, on the Gospels. Charles II made his oath while holding the Bible in his hand. The Bible was presented to Elizabeth II jointly by representatives of the churches of England and Scotland after the recitation of the oath.

 ## The Anointing

After taking the oath the monarch is prepared for receiving unction. In the Middle Ages, certainly from the end of the fourteenth century but maybe earlier, two special tunic-like shirts, one of white lawn the other of royal red tartaryn (silk thought to be imported from Tartary), were worn by the monarch for this part of the ceremony. The king was divested of his outer robes, which were then offered at the altar. Both shirts were custom-made with wide openings before, behind and on the shoulders and a wide opening at front and back extending to the middle of the thigh. The king's under garments, also traditionally of crimson, had openings to match those of the coronation shirts to facilitate anointing. Edward I may have worn the wrong shirt for his coronation in 1274 for it seems the Archbishop may have had to tear it in order to reach the parts to be anointed. One crimson shirt became the customary anointing attire at later coronations. A queen-consort's equivalent of the

The sovereign waits in readiness for the anointing. The wearing of white, denoting purity of purpose and spirit, was a fourteenth-century custom revived by James I and Charles I. Their predecessors had worn a red shirt beneath their rich red outer robes. A canopy is held over the sovereign during this most sacred part of the ceremony; the four bearers seen here holding Queen Elizabeth's canopy are Knights of the Garter. Like George VI before her, Queen Elizabeth was anointed in the old order of hands, breast and head.

royal shirt of red silk was a close-fitting garment of red taffeta. Both James I and Charles I risked offending Puritan sentiment by reverting to the fourteenth-century practice of wearing a white coronation shirt instead of a red one. For her anointing, Elizabeth II wore a white shift-like garment, a modern version of the be-ribboned shirt made for the coronation of Charles II, and a pleated skirt beneath her Parliamentary robes.

The antiphon 'Veni Creator Spiritus' is sung during the preliminaries to anointing. The oil used for anointing, referred to as the oil of gladness in the New Testament, is then poured into an anointing spoon and applied while the choir sing the antiphon of 'Zadok the Priest', which has been the traditional accompaniment to this part of the coronation ritual since the tenth century. The anointing spoon is first mentioned at the coronation of James I. The medieval method of anointing was by dipping the fingers in the oil and making the sign of the cross on each part of the body. Richard III was probably the first monarch to depart from the practice of receiving unction whilst prostrate before the altar. He knelt. This prescription was followed by Henry VII, Henry VIII and Charles I. Post-Restoration the practice has been for the monarch to remain seated during unction. Four Knights of the Garter hold a pall over the monarch during this part of the ceremony.

Before the coronation of Henry I in 1100 English kings were anointed in the manner of bishops, on the crown of the head. The order compiled for Henry's coronation stated that the breast, shoulder-blades, hands and elbows should also be anointed. This change in the ritual may have been brought about by a dispute between Henry and the then Archbishop of Canterbury, Anselm, regarding the question of whether the King, because he was both king and priest, had as much power over the Church as he did the laity. Canterbury was at this point in the history of the coronation responsible for compiling the orders for the ceremony. The Church, keen to disabuse Henry and future monarchs of the idea of royal supremacy in both lay and clerical matters, introduced this change as a way of making a clear distinction between the two offices. The new order also stated that the king should no longer receive the holiest form of

The gold ampulla used to hold the consecrated anointing oil or chrism was made for the coronation of Charles II in 1661. The anointing spoon dates from the second half of the twelfth century. The first mention of the use of such a spoon is at the coronation of James I in 1603. The original ampulla, lost in 1649, was made of stone and small enough to be worn as a pendant. The reason for reinterpreting this article as a larger vessel on a plinth is not recorded. The reason for its eagle form may derive from a legend describing the vision of St Thomas. In this the Virgin Mary gave to St Thomas a golden eagle to house the small stone phial of oil with which he was to anoint a new line of English kings.

unction, anointing by chrism, a mixture of oil and balsam which is then sanctified by being blessed. It is thought, however, that chrism was rarely, if ever, omitted at this time; the one exception may have been King Stephen's coronation in 1136. Chrism was usually reserved for the head, while holy oil (unmixed oil that has been blessed) was used for anointing the other parts of the body. The relative status of the two oils was denoted by the style of cruet used to contain them; the precious chrism was housed in silver-gilt, the holy oil in plain silver.

England's claim to France was reflected symbolically in the form of anointing performed for Henry IV at his coronation in 1399. Henry was anointed in the manner of French kings, between the shoulder blades, in addition to on the breast, shoulders, elbows, head and hands.

Perhaps the most puzzling anointing was that of Edward VI, who received both chrism and holy oil on his breast, elbows, wrists, crown and, uniquely, the soles of his feet. His very thorough anointing was performed by the Archbishop of Canterbury, Thomas Cranmer, who in his address to the King at the coronation strongly attacked the sacramental nature of the traditional consecration and unction and denied that popes had the power to make kings. The manner of Edward's anointing is surprising given the general playing down of the notion of the king needing any additional sanctity.

Since the coronation of William and Mary in 1689, most monarchs have been anointed on the head, breast and hands. Two notable exceptions to this have been William IV and Queen Victoria, both of whom were anointed on the head and hands. Queens-consort were initially anointed on the head only and from the late fourteenth century on the head and breast. Several have been anointed on the head only; for example, Queens Adelaide and Mary, the wives of William IV and George V respectively.

After the anointing oil has been applied, it is dabbed dry on the monarch's body. At medieval coronations as much of the oil as possible was preserved on the body, especially on the monarch's head, from where it was intended that the unction should sink in 'to his inner parts'. Even in the twentieth century an awareness of the symbolic significance of anointing has not been lost. Queen Alexandra, wife of Edward VII, was so concerned that the oil should penetrate the thickness of her false hair piece that she asked the Archbishop of Canterbury to ensure a thorough anointing. Mindful of his request, he applied the oil with a rather too liberal hand. The 'look of anguish' that accompanied the Queen's awareness of the liquid dribbling down her nose was the only sign, according to one of her pall-bearers, the Duchess of Marlborough, of her concern at this unfortunate consequence of a well-intentioned request.

It used to be customary to place a linen cloth on the monarch's head and cover it with a special cap, called a *pileum regale*, to keep it in place. Later, from the coronation of Edward III in 1327, a linen coif (a close-fitting cap, probably with ties under the chin) came to replace the cloth and cap. The monarch's hair remained covered in this fashion for eight days. At the end of this time the hair was washed in the royal chapel as part of a ritual called dealbation. A Mass was said in the presence of the king after which the officiating bishop, or the Abbot of Westminster, removed the covering, which was then burnt, and washed the king's hair: lukewarm white wine was used for Henry VI's dealbation. Finally, the king received a circlet of gold which he had to wear for the rest of the day in token of his cleansing.

From the coronation of Henry IV (1399) the oil used for anointing English monarchs took on a special significance. Henry was the first king to be anointed with oil allegedly from the ampulla of St Thomas à Becket. The cult that had grown up round Becket since his murder at the hands of four of Henry II's knights in 1170 was given official clerical sanction by Becket's canonization three years later. According to the Dominican friar who produced the ampulla before Edward II, Becket had received a phial of holy oil from the Virgin Mary at some time during his six-year exile in France. This was to be used to anoint future kings of

England, beginning with the fifth king in succession from Henry II, then reigning. The oil was presented to Edward II, the fifth king, in time for his coronation but Edward and his council favoured instead the traditional holy oil and declined to use it. (Nine years into an unhappy reign that would end with his murder, Edward asked Pope John XXII whether he could be anointed again, this time with Becket's oil. The Pope, reluctant to grant second unction and uncertain of the origins of the ampulla and its contents, dissuaded the King.)

The ampulla then found its way into a locked chest in the royal treasury before it was discovered by Richard II, after his coronation. Richard found the stone ampulla inside a gold eagle while he was going through the possessions left to him by his ancestors. Like Edward II, he too enquired about the possibility of a second anointing with Becket's oil; and, like Edward, he too was refused, this time by the Archbishop of Canterbury, Thomas Arundel. Richard wore the ampulla suspended round his neck as a pendant during the ill-judged trip to Ireland which gave his rival, Henry Bolingbroke (the future Henry IV), the opportunity to oust him. On his return, the deposed King relinquished the ampulla to Arundel, now one of Henry's strongest supporters, with the acknowledgement that 'so noble a sacrament was another's due'.

The oil from Becket's ampulla continued to be used until the coronation of Mary Tudor in 1553. The Catholic Mary believed that the oil had lost its sanctity because it had been used at the coronation of her half-brother, Edward VI, a champion of Protestantism. She sent to the court of her father-in-law, the Emperor Charles V, in Brussels for a fresh, uncontaminated supply. Mary's half-sister, Elizabeth I, reverted to tradition, as did the last monarch to use Becket's oil, James I.

For Charles I's coronation, in 1625, fresh oil was compounded by the king's physicians and blessed by Archbishop Laud. What prompted the order for new oil is not known – the oil in Becket's ampulla may have run out or Charles and his advisers may have thought better of risking Puritan criticism by using such a relic of superstition. The recipe promised a sweeter-smelling oil than Becket's brew, which, according to Elizabeth I's description of it to her maids, had the consistency of 'grease' and 'smelt ill'. The ingredients for Charles's oil were oils of orange and jasmine, distilled roses, cinammon, oil of bean, extract of flowers of benzoin, and ambergris, musk and civet. Fresh anointing oil has been prepared for each subsequent coronation.

 ### The Delivery of the Insignia

After the anointing the monarch is prepared for receiving the regalia and invested in a colobium, similar to the dalmatic worn by clerics, a supertunica (a long overgarment), stole and mantle; the four corners of the mantle represented to medieval minds the subjection of the four quarters of the world to God, who alone could grant a happy reign. These garments are the modern equivalents of the medieval St Edward's robes.

The centuries-long tradition of investing the king with St Edward's robes was broken at the Protestant-influenced coronation of Edward VI in 1547 and not re-adopted until the coronation of James I in 1603. The mingling of priestly attire, symbolized by St Edward's robes, with his own regal dress provided a visual expression of James's belief in his headship of the Church and the divine right by which he ruled.

Cloth-of-gold buskins were among the items designated as St Edward's vestments for the king to don before receiving the regalia. Charles I almost succeeded in destroying these by now very venerable and treasured possessions prematurely by insisting, against the advice of Archbishop Laud, of putting them on over the shoes he was wearing.

Beginning with the coronation of Charles II in 1661, after the loss of the original St Edward's vestments in 1649, new robes were made for each

Below: The Sword of Offering is either girded on the sovereign or grasped by him or her before being offered at the high altar. The senior earl present will then redeem it from the altar at a cost of 100 shillings and bear it, unsheathed, before the monarch for the rest of the ceremony.

coronation and then surrendered to the Abbey afterwards. This practice ceased with the coronation of Queen Victoria in 1838. George V and all his successors have chosen to wear the splendid mantle and supertunica made for George IV's coronation in 1821.

The task of delivering the insignia was initially performed by representatives of those who had elected the king, namely high clerics and great nobles. It then became wholly the office of churchmen, until the coronation of Edward VI in 1547. The Archbishop assisted only in the

THE CORONATION CEREMONY AND THE CROWN JEWELS

THE CORONATION CEREMONY AND THE CROWN JEWELS

crowning and did not deliver the other items of the regalia. This prescription was maintained after the Reformation and up until the Commonwealth. The ceremonials devised for James I's coronation in 1603, although in some respects marking a reversion to medieval practice, did not restore this formerly important part of the Archbishop's role in the ritual. In all post-Commonwealth coronation ceremonies the delivery of the regalia has been performed by the officiating archbishop or bishop, assisted by royal officers, such as the Lord Great Chamberlain and the Master of the Jewel House.

The number of insignia and the order in which they have been delivered to the king has changed through the centuries. Under the orders of coronation devised in the ninth century the king received only a sceptre and staff and a 'galeum', a crown or helmet-crown, which was placed on his head by all the bishops present. These main ornaments have since been supplemented by spurs, sword, bracelets or armillas, ring, stole, mantle and gloves.

The spurs are delivered to the monarch and then returned to the altar. The form of delivery has changed through the ages. Up to and including the coronation of Charles I the spurs were actually fastened on the heels of the monarch. Subsequently they have been touched to the heels of kings and merely presented to queens-regnant.

Similarly, the way of delivering the Sword of Offering has tended to differ according to the sex of the monarch, although there have been exceptions to this neat generalization. Victoria and Elizabeth II, for example, grasped the sword instead of having it girded on them, the usual prescription for kings. Queen Anne, Mary Tudor and Elizabeth I were girded, the last with a shoulder-belt. William and Mary grasped the sword jointly. William's namesake, William IV, seems to have been the only other king not to be girded.

A special spoken formula accompanies the delivery of each ornament. The medieval formula for receiving the sword remained the same for centuries: 'and with the sword he should know that the whole kingdom is

Left: The sovereign is invested with special robes after the anointing and immediately prior to receiving the ornaments. King George VI, wearing George IV's cloth-of-gold vestments, is about to put on the traditional 'rich gloves' before receiving the sceptres. The gloves are the traditional gift of the lords of the Manor of Worksop.

THE CORONATION CEREMONY AND THE CROWN JEWELS

commended to his care to be ruled with equity, to the destruction of iniquity and to the defence of Holy Church and of his people'. For the coronation of Charles II, the sword was delivered with the words 'Receive the sword from the hands of the bishops', it was then girded on by the Lord Great Chamberlain to the invocation of the Archbishop.

The girding on of the sword could be a hazardous business. George VI, for example, narrowly missed being dealt a blow with the hilt as his Lord Great Chamberlain ham-fistedly wrestled with the apparatus of sword and girdle. It is unlikely, however, that risk of injury prompted some monarchs to gird themselves, for example, Richard III and probably the Henrys V, VII and VIII.

The sword delivered to the monarch is offered at the altar. It is then redeemed by the senior earl present and borne naked before the monarch for the rest of the ceremony. In the early fourteenth century the symbolic meaning of this act of redeeming the sword was explained in the notion of the king's strength and powers deriving from God. In the Middle Ages the custom was established of paying one hundred shillings to redeem the sword. This sum is still given on behalf of the monarch by the nobleman who redeems the sword.

The delivery of the sword is followed by the bracelets (if used), the armil, or royal stole (see page 52), the mantle and orb. The orb is usually returned to the altar after delivery and re-presented to the monarch at the Recess before the final procession.

The ring is delivered next. When this item was first delivered, in the tenth century, it was given immediately after the unction. From the early twelfth century it was given after the crown and before the sceptre and rod; the order followed at every coronation up to and including that of Charles II. James II received the ring after the delivery of the sword.

The order for the coronation of Richard III (1483) stated that the ring should be put on the fourth finger of the right hand. This stipulation changed to the fourth finger of the left hand for the coronation of Edward

The sovereign receives the Sceptre with Cross first, in the right hand, followed by the Sceptre with Dove, in the left. The former signifies the sovereign's temporal power under the cross, the latter the monarch's spiritual role.

THE CORONATION CEREMONY AND THE CROWN JEWELS

THE CORONATION CEREMONY AND THE CROWN JEWELS

106

VI in 1547, a practice followed at the coronation of James I in 1603. Charles I and all of his successors have reverted to the fifteenth-century instruction.

A misapprehension on the part of Rundell's, the royal goldsmiths, as to what constituted the fourth finger resulted in a very painful experience for Queen Victoria at her coronation in 1838. Rundell's counted the forefinger as the first digit instead of the thumb. The Archbishop of Canterbury had to force the ring made to fit her little finger onto the larger digit next to it. After the ceremony the Queen had to soak her swollen finger in iced water in order to remove the ring.

The monarch dons a pair of gloves before receiving the two sceptres. The Sceptre with Cross is placed in the monarch's right hand, the Sceptre with Dove in the left one.

 The Crowning

Seated on the Coronation Chair – called St Edward's Chair, this has been used at all coronations since the Restoration and clasping the two sceptres, the monarch now awaits delivery of the ultimate symbol of kingship, the crown. Medieval chroniclers appropriated Roman symbolism of the

Far left: The Primate of All England, the Archbishop of Canterbury, raises St Edward's Crown before placing it on the sovereign's head. Queen Elizabeth took the precaution of clearly marking the front of the crown with two silver stars so that the Archbishop could not mistake it for the back.

Below: The Archbishop who crowned Queen Victoria was the last of the great prelates to wear a wig. The Queen was crowned not with St Edward's Crown, as has been the practice since King George V, but with a new Imperial State Crown adorned with diamonds and precious stones from George I's state crown. The Queen retained her coronation vestments (which are now on display in the Museum of London), bringing to an end the practice of giving them to the Dean of Westminster as a perquisite.

THE CORONATION CEREMONY AND THE CROWN JEWELS

The first intention of Edward I when he commissioned the coronation chair was to use it as a means of incorporating the Stone of Scone into the coronation service. The Stone, traditionally the stone on which the kings of Scotland sat at the time of their coronation, was the most precious of the symbols of Scottish royalty which Edward brought back as trophies from the campaign of 1296. Together with the regalia, royal plate and jewels of the defeated John de Balliol, it was a potent reminder of the Scottish claim to be an independent kingdom.

The chair was originally to be made of latten, an alloy similar to brass. In 1297, however, Edward decided that it should be made of wood instead of costly metal. Edward had perhaps reflected on the wisdom of validating the stone as a symbol of Scottish kingship by placing it in a costly chair on which 'the kings of England and Scotland may sit . . . on the day of their coronation'. In the inventory of 1306/7, the last of his reign, Edward wanted it known that the chair was sent to Westminster Abbey only 'in perpetual memory of his achievement'.

By 1301 the chair was in place beside St Edward's altar in the Abbey. At this time a new foot or step was added under the chair to raise it higher. This was replaced in the early sixteenth century by four small gilt lions. (Lions, known as leopards in the Middle Ages, were incorporated into the design of all medieval thrones because they were the principal emblems of the throne of Solomon described in the Bible.) The chair was transformed into a royal chair at some time during the fourteenth century, with a covering of gesso inset with mosaic ornament of glass and gilded. Even after this transformation, however, the purpose of the chair was uncertain.

THE CORONATION CEREMONY AND THE CROWN JEWELS

110

crown as an ensign of victory. The arch above the circlet on the imperial type of crown signifies the ocean that was said to divide the world, a world that the emperor rules.

In the modern coronation ceremony the Archbishop of Canterbury alone places the crown on the monarch's head. This was also established practice until the coronation of Edward VI, although there are two recorded instances of medieval kings (Richard I and Edward II) partly assigning the assumption of the crown to himself; Richard took the crown from the altar and gave it to the Archbishop, who placed it on the King's head. Edward VI was crowned jointly by the Archbishop and Lord Protector Somerset. Three crowns were in turn placed on his head: St Edward's Crown, an imperial crown and a small personal crown. Trumpets sounded before each crowning. The coronation of Edward's successor, Mary Tudor, brought a reversion to the practice of the Archbishop alone crowning the monarch, although the crown was brought to him by the Duke of Norfolk and the Bishop of Winchester. The one-legged Marquis of Anglesey, a veteran of Waterloo, came perilously close to dropping the crown when he alone had the honour of bringing it to the Archbishop at George IV's coronation.

Before his coronation in 1937 George VI arranged for a length of red thread to be tied to one of the jewels on the front of St Edward's Crown to ensure that the Archbishop could not fail to put the crown on the right way round. By the time the Archbishop came to crown the king the thread had disappeared – removed by 'some officious person', in the opinion of the Archbishop – and he made the best of the situation. Although the crown stayed on his head, George was convinced that he had worn it back to front. Elizabeth II, no doubt mindful of her father's experience, had the front of the crown marked unambiguously with two silver stars.

The point of crowning was described by Queen Victoria as 'a most beautiful impressive moment'. 'Chips' Channon recaptured that moment at George VI's coronation in a memorable description – 'the shaft of sunlight, catching the king's golden tunic as he sat for the crowning; the

Queen Victoria described the crowning as 'a most beautiful, impressive moment'. The spectacle involves the congregation, the peers and peeresses among them putting on their coronets as the sovereign is crowned. At the coronation of Edward VII, in 1902, the temporary electric lights installed in the Abbey were switched on, literally highlighting the climax of the ceremony. 'The shouts, which were very great, the drums, the trumpets, the firing of the guns, all at the same instant, rendered the spectacle most imposing', Queen Victoria recorded in her diary.

THE CORONATION CEREMONY AND THE CROWN JEWELS

kneeling bishops drawn up like a flight of geese in deploy position; and then the loveliest moment of all, the swirl when the peeresses put on their coronets: a thousand white gloved arms, sparkling with jewels, lifting their tiny coronets'. The peers, too, doffed their caps of maintenance with their encircling coronets and great shouts of 'God save the King' rang out amidst the sound of drums, trumpets and cannon fire.

 ## Inthronization and Homage

During the inthronization which follows the crowning the Archbishop exhorts the monarch to 'Stand firm and hold fast' in a prayer which first became part of the ceremonials for coronation in the early Middle Ages. The prayer defines the sources of the king's royal estate as his birth, God and the clergy, and calls on him to protect the last-mentioned and be the intermediary between them and his people.

While still seated on the throne the monarch receives the homage, a demonstration of loyalty, from the assembled nobles and clergy. At Henry V's coronation in 1413 the great nobles caused great surprise by performing this ritual before the King had taken the oath. They made it plain, however, that their action should not be taken as a precedent.

The homage has taken several forms over the centuries. In the late fourteenth century the great nobles gathered round the throne and stretched out their hands to offer support to the king and his crown. The evidence suggests that this particular form was borrowed from the French coronation ritual. At Edward VI's coronation both Lord Protector Somerset and Archbishop Cranmer knelt down and kissed the King's right foot and then, holding their hands between the King's, kissed the King's left cheek. Other nobles, lay and clergy, then made their homage together after each of them had kissed the King's left cheek.

The procedure at James I's ceremony marked a shift of emphasis. The earls put on their caps to do their homage while the barons approached the King uncovered. Approaching the King one by one, the noblemen bowed at the foot of the steps to the throne, then went up, knelt on a

The sovereign sits on St Edward's Chair, bearing the emblems of majesty, before moving to the throne on the upper level of the 'theatre' for the inthronization and homage.

THE CORONATION CEREMONY AND THE CROWN JEWELS

cushion and kissed the King's right hand and either touched or kissed his crown. The King's favourite, the Earl of Pembroke, kissed the King's face in preference to the crown and received a playful slap from his amused sovereign.

At Charles II's coronation the Archbishop knelt and spoke the words of homage first and then kissed the King's cheek, as did all the bishops after him. The clergy were followed by the Duke of York, later James II, who removed his coronet to swear fealty, which was greeted by the sound of drums, trumpets and shouts. The nobles then approached in their various degrees, a representative or representatives of each rank paying homage on behalf of their peers. Trumpets and drums sounded between the homage of each degree. The Duke of York returned again, removed his coronet and touched St Edward's Crown on his brother's head. After James the nobility came to touch the crown.

Far left: The Archbishop and bishops are the first to pay homage to the sovereign, followed by members of the royal family and a representative or representatives of each rank of the nobility. The Duke of Edinburgh is seen here paying homage to Queen Elizabeth.

Below: The coronation of James II and his consort, Mary of Modena, in 1685. The King's throne is set on a higher platform than the Queen's to signify his superiority; as joint-sovereigns, King William and Queen Mary would be seated on platforms of equal height at their coronation in 1689.

THE CORONATION CEREMONY AND THE CROWN JEWELS

The Coronation Ceremony and the Crown Jewels

The coronation of Queen Victoria in 1838 established the current practice of the prelates and peers touching the crown and kissing the monarch's hand instead of his or her left cheek.

During this very long process a General Pardon used to be read on the south, west and north of the 'theatre'; this practice was discontinued in the nineteenth century. In the Middle Ages it became customary for the Treasurer of the King's Household to fling coronation medals of gold and silver among the congregation. The ensuing scramble became a minor feature of coronation until 1838, when the decision was taken to abandon this part of the proceedings. Instead, it was decided to present medals to the people who had performed duties at the coronation.

 ### Recess and Closing Procession

Queen Elizabeth II took Communion with her husband and made the traditional oblation of an altar cloth and a gold brick weighing 1lb at the altar before retiring to St Edward's Chapel to prepare for the closing procession. (This offering is made because, according to the medieval notion, the monarch must not 'appere voide ne empte in the presence and sight of thi lord god'.)

Victoria described the Chapel as a 'small dark place immediately behind the altar'. She was shocked by what she found there: 'what was called an altar . . . covered with sandwiches, bottles of wine, etc'. Given the length of time the clerical attendants had to spend in the Abbey, it is little wonder they came well provisioned. If wished, the monarch could at this point in the proceedings break the fast necessitated by the taking of Communion. In the privacy of the Chapel the monarch takes off the dalmatic and supertunica and dons purple velvet robes. St Edward's Crown is removed and a state crown placed on the monarch's head by the Archbishop. The Orb and Sceptre with Cross are re-presented to the monarch for the final procession; Charles I had his sceptre and the rod of St Edward borne before him. The swords – Curtana, the two Swords of Justice and the Sword of Offering – are also carried, unsheathed, before the monarch.

At the conclusion of the homage the sovereign leaves the throne and returns to the chair of state and faldstool to the side of the altar for the Communion service. The traditional oblation of a gold ingot is incorporated in the service. A new prayer was written for Queen Elizabeth's consort, the Duke of Edinburgh, in 1953.

Overleaf: The sovereign emerges from St Edward's Chapel – 'a small dark place immediately behind the altar,' according to Queen Victoria – after the Recess to take part in the closing procession out of the Abbey. Queen Elizabeth is wearing purple velvet robes and bearing the state crown on her head and in her hands the orb (re-presented to her at the Recess) and the Sceptre with Cross.

THE CORONATION CEREMONY AND THE CROWN JEWELS

118

THE CORONATION CEREMONY AND THE CROWN JEWELS

119

When St Edward's robes were still in use, these were formally handed back to the Abbot of Westminster during the Recess. The sceptres were the only items of St Edward's regalia retained by the monarch, and these were relinquished to the Abbot after the coronation feast. The decision not to allow the monarch to leave the Abbey still wearing St Edward's vestments was made after the coronation of Richard II in 1377. One of the buskins had been lost as the eleven-year-old Richard was carried bodily through the large throng of people gathered around the gateway to the Palace by Sir Simon Burley, the King's tutor.

Medieval kings and queens would return to the scaffold after putting on their robes of estate in the traverse by St Edward's shrine. They would then chat with their lords and ladies while they waited for the Archbishop and clergy to change their Mass pontificals for ordinary robes.

Celia Fiennes, who attended the coronation of Queen Anne in 1702, wrote that the Queen made her way to the door of the Abbey 'with obligeing lookes and bows to all that saluted her and were spectatours, which were prodigious numbers in scaffolds built in the Abby and all the streetes'. Anne was then chaired to her coronation feast in Westminster Hall.

 ## The Feast

The last monarch to have a coronation feast was Queen Victoria's uncle, George IV. George's feast was in keeping with every other aspect of his coronation. Huge quantities of food were provided. Three hundred and thirty-six people alone were catered for at the cold buffet tables which lined the sides of Westminster Hall. More tables were laid in the law courts outside the Hall and in rooms inside the Houses of Parliament. The hot dishes included 160 tureens of soup (eighty containing turtle), 160 dishes of fish (turbot, trout and salmon), 160 hot joints of venison, beef, mutton and veal, the same number of dishes with vegetables and 480 sauce boats with lobster, butter and mint sauces. Aside from the ingredients used in the desserts, 7,442lb of beef, 7,133lb of veal,

Left: The sovereign making the journey back to Buckingham Palace. Queen Victoria remembered this part of the day thus, . . . 'we proceeded the same way as we came – the crowds if possible having increased. The enthusiasm, affection and loyalty was really touching.'

The weather was not kind to the thousands who turned out to cheer Queen Elizabeth II. Many of them had braved the rain and stayed out all night to secure places along the processional route. Queen Elizabeth's coronation was the first to be televised. The cornation of her predecessor, George VI, had been broadcast and parts of the ceremony filmed for the newsreels. Television and film cameras had also been set up outside Buckingham Palace and along the processional route.

The traditional banquet has not been a feature of coronations since 1821. The practice since then has been for guests to be entertained at various smaller gatherings in the capital. Members of the Commons and Lords and their wives, for example, would dine at the Houses of Parliament after the ceremony; and dignitaries from overseas would be entertained at Westminster Palace by the Government Hospitality Committee. This illustration depicts the lunch for royals and nobles given by King George VI and Queen Elizabeth at Buckingham Palace in 1937.

2,474lb of mutton, 75 quarters of lamb, 5 saddles of lamb, 160 lambs' sweetbreads, 389 cowheels, 300 calves' feet, 250lb of suet, 160 geese, 720 pullets and capons, 1,610 chickens, 520 fowls for stock, 1,730lb of bacon, 550lb of lard, 912lb of butter and 8,400 eggs were used in the making of the feast.

In their eagerness to make in-roads into this gargantuan offering, the City aldermen broke ranks to seat themselves at table, only to be marshalled back into line by the Heralds. However, by some wizardry the aldermen managed to feast very well on turtle and venison while the peers, the rightful recipients of these and other hot collations, were served only cold food.

At the coronation feast for Charles II the stands ranged along the sides of the Hall were packed with onlookers who tried as best they could to charm food from the tables below. Pepys was successful to the order of four rabbits, a pullet and some bread, which he shared with his friends.

The coronation feast of the early Middle Ages seems to have been a more dignified affair, and for the king a necessity after the hours spent fasting in preparation for taking Communion. At the feast for the tenth-century King Edgar, 'there was no sound of the trumpet or of the minstrel's pipe' and men drank 'only as much as their age and capacity allowed'.

The banquet held after Edward I's coronation in 1274 lasted a fortnight, in emulation of Solomon's fortnight-long feast. Throughout the day of Edward's coronation the conduit in Cheapside ran with red and white wine 'for all who wished to drink', thus setting a precedent that would be maintained until the seventeenth century.

From the coronation of Henry IV onwards (1399) some ceremony became a regular part of the coronation feast. Henry, for example, sat in royal estate framed by two swords and two sceptres. The order of the coronation feast for Henry and the other Lancastrian kings was particularly solemn. Although invitations to the feast were not restricted to noblemen, and clerks of the royal chancery together with worthy commoners were admitted, the king shared his table with few, if any. Henry VI, for example, allowed only a cardinal, the Chancellor and the Archbishop of Rheims to dine with him.

By the time of Henry VIII the feast had become more obviously celebratory in character. At the feast for Anne Boleyn, for example, the Duke of Suffolk, as High Steward, and the Earl Marshal, Lord William Howard (deputizing for his brother, Lord Arundel), rode up and down the Hall on their horses encouraging the lords, ladies and City dignitaries to eat and drink. The service was said to have been astonishingly quick and efficient, and the food delicious. The Mayor of London was served with thirty-three dishes in two courses. The Queen was served twenty-two dishes at her second course and thirty at her third. Trumpeters standing in the window embrasure at the lower end of the Hall played melodiously while the diners enjoyed the fare.

Elaborate dishes in sculptural or architectural form were devised for the coronation feast from quite early days. The general cult of heraldry and

THE CORONATION CEREMONY AND THE CROWN JEWELS

symbolic devices which flourished in the fourteenth century had a great influence on all the arts of the later Middle Ages. At the coronation banquet of Catherine of France, the new wife of Henry V, in February 1421, the union of England and France as symbolized by the couple's marriage was celebrated in a succession of allusive dishes. For example, a 'leeke lombard' (a sort of jelly) was decorated with the SS livery collars of the House of Lancaster and the broom-cod device of Catherine's father, Charles VI. The third course had a marzipan of St. Catherine of Alexandria, the queen's patron saint, among angels with an inscription proclaiming that the war between England and France had been ended by the marriage of Henry and Catherine. At the feast of Henry's son, Henry VI, in 1429 the Lancastrian claim to rule both England and France would be reiterated in such devices as the patron saints St Denis and St George presenting Henry to the child Jesus, who holds a crown in each hand.

One of the most colourful features of the coronation feast was the appearance of the King's Champion to issue a public challenge to any who denied the king's right to the throne. The office of Champion came into existence before 1327 – precisely when is not clear – and at this time the knight rode ahead of the opening procession. At the coronation of Richard II in 1377 the Champion, Sir John Dymoke – whose family had secured the right to perform the service – appeared at the end of the Mass only to be told to perform his service at the coronation feast, which he duly did. The Champion's entrance was made as dramatic as possible. At the coronation feast of George III, for example, the Champion rode through the Gothic archway to the Hall clad in a suit of white armour – provided by the Tower Armouries – and mounted on a white horse. James II's Champion rather spoilt the effect of the pagaent by falling flat on his face after he had dismounted to kiss the monarch's hand.

At first, the Champion received a fee of the horse and armour only if he faced a challenge. If there was none – and there is no record of one – then the king had to decide whether or not to give the horse and armour. By the time of the coronation of George III in 1761 it had become customary for the Champion to be lent a horse and armour and for his fee to be a modest gilt cup. John Dymoke, the then Champion, had exalted ideas

The King's Champion performing his role for the last time, at the coronation banquet of George IV in 1821. The Champion's challenge was issued by one or more heralds. Originally attendants on their lords at tournaments, heralds first appeared in coronation in the late fourteenth century. Their thanks for largesse became part of the ceremonial of the banquet during the fifteenth century.

Other services performed at the coronation banquet included bringing the king his first drink, a cup of wine. This was the right of the lord of the manor or Wymondley, who retained the silver-gilt cup as his fee for the service. Not all the offerings were so pleasurable – Charles II, for example, wisely refrained from consuming a mess of gruel (the traditional dilligrout) presented to him by a Mr Leigh of Addington.

The principal lighting provided in Westminster Hall for the banquet of George IV comprised 2,000 candles in assorted holders supplemented by gas lamps. The latter, it seems, had a disastrous wilting effect on the hair-dos of ladies unfortunate enough to be seated close to them.

about his position, however, and insisted on retaining the horse and armour. The authorities prevented future procurements of this kind by hiring horse and armour from outside; for the coronation of George IV the horse was hired from Astley's Circus and the suit of armour from an antiques dealer. Since George IV's coronation the role of the Champion has been reduced to that of a standard bearer.

The monarch's departure from the feast was the signal for the spectators to descend on the royal tables and help themselves to the leftovers. This tradition dated from medieval times, when it was customary to give the leavings to the poor. At the coronation feast of George IV the crowd also helped themselves to some of the small items of plate on the royal table. The Lord Great Chamberlain prevented the plunder of the large plate by ordering its removal. Fearing that the many people clamouring for admittance might not, if allowed in, confine themselves to the traditional perquisite of the food on the tables, the officials inside the Hall summoned troops to keep them out. So great was the pandemonium in the streets that the guests spent hours awaiting their carriages. George had made his farewells at about eight o'clock, bringing the official banquet to an end. The last of his guests would not be reunited with their carriages until three o'clock the next morning.

Samuel Pepys made his way home after enjoying the ad-hoc meal and the music, especially the 'viollins'. The day produced only one disappointment for him: a cloudburst put paid to the firework display. The rain had not, though, managed to extinguish the large bonfires which had been lit in celebration of the new reign. The City 'had a light like a glory round it'.

Queen Victoria spent an equally enjoyable evening, banqueting at Buckingham Palace. She would, she confided to her journal, 'ever remember this day as the proudest of my life'.

THE CORONATION CEREMONY AND THE CROWN JEWELS

THE CORONATION CEREMONY AND THE CROWN JEWELS

Index

Opposite: *Popular
entertainments in London on
coronation day have been many
and various, with the
traditional firework display
providing a fitting finale. The
splendour of the Hyde Park
display devised by Sir William
Congreve for the coronation of
George IV in 1821 can be
gauged by its cost of
£8,235. 19s. 11d. Even the
relatively modest coronation of
William IV – dubbed the 'half-
crownation' – had a 'grand
discharge of fireworks' between
nine and eleven o'clock at night.
The 'summer theatres' at
Vauxhall and elsewhere were
opened free of charge to the
public. In the evening of the
coronation of King George V in
1911 the royal parks were filled
with revellers; Green Park
remained open all night. Shortly
before ten o'clock the Prime
Minister's eight-year-old son,
Anthony Asquith, telephoned an
order to Crystal Palace to fire the
rocket that signalled the lighting
of great bonfires all over the
kingdom.*

THE CORONATION CEREMONY AND THE CROWN JEWELS

Acknowledgements

Illustrations are reproduced by kind permission of the following: *The Royal Collection, St James's Palace* © *Her Majesty The Queen:* pages 1 (The Triumphs of Caesar, Canvas IX, Andrea Mantegna, Hampton Court Palace), 8–9 (The Field of Cloth of Gold, artist unknown), 11 (Charles I and Henrietta Maria with The Liberal Arts, Gerald von Honthorst), 38 (portrait of Queen Victoria, 1899, Jean-Joseph-Benjamin Constant), 68 (William of Orange landing at Torbay, artist unknown), 124 (Coronation Banquet of George IV, Jones). *Bridgeman Art Library*: pages 3 (Mercy: David Spareth Saul's Life, Richard Dadd, The Fine Art Society, London), 15 (Henry III being crowned, Cotton Vit. A X III fol, miniature, British Museum, London), 40 left (portrait of Edward VII, Sir Luke Fildes, Crown Estate Commissioners, London), 44 (portrait of Richard II, Westminster Abbey), 48 (oil, Thanksgiving Service for George V and Queen Mary, 1935, Frank Salisbury, Guildhall Art Gallery, London), 60–1 (oil, procession of Charles II to Westminster from the Tower of London, 1661, Dirck Stoop, Private Collection), 66 (Coronation Procession of Edward VI, Society of Antiquaries, London), 83 (George IV in Coronation Robes wearing a Cap of Estate, Sir George Naylor, engraved by E. Scrivenor, Guildhall Library, Corporation of London), 107 (The Coronation of Queen Victoria, artist unknown, Bradford Art Galleries and Museums), 122 (Coronation Lunch for George VI and Queen Elizabeth 1937, Frank Salisbury, Guildhall Art Gallery, Corporation of London). *Angelo Hornak Library*: pages 5 (reliquary bust, 14th cent., The Treasury, Aachen Cathedral), 6 (wooden screen, *c.*1500, St Catherine's Ludham, Norfolk), 13 (bronze effigy of Edward III, possibly by John Orchard, Westminster Abbey, courtesy of the Dean and Chapter, Westminster Abbey), 16 (bronze effigy of Richard II by Nicholas Broker and Godrey Prest, Westminster Abbey, courtesy of the Dean and Chapter, Westminster Abbey), 56 (view of the nave, York Minster, courtesy of the Chapter Clerk, York Minster), 57 (bronze tomb effigy of Henry III, Westminster Abbey, courtesy of the Dean and Chapter, Westminster Abbey), 65 (Shrine of King Edward the Confessor, Westminster Abbey, courtesy of the Dean and Chapter, Westminster Abbey), 74 (The Great Hall, the Palace of Westminster, courtesy of the Gentleman Usher of the Black Rod), 96 (stained glass, *c.*1220, Henry II doing penance at the tomb of Thomas à Becket in 1174, Trinity Chapel, Canterbury Cathedral, courtesy of the Dean and Chapter, Canterbury Cathedral). *The Mansell Collection*: pages 12 (engraving, The Royal Gift of Healing, from John Brown, Adenochoiradelogia, 1684), 17 (engraving, The Tower and Its Liberties, Brayley, Londiniana), 18 (engraving, HESP, Vol II), 20 (engraving), 70–1 (engraving, Coronation Procession of Mary, Consort of James II, from Sandford), 78 bottom (engraving, Coronation Procession of James II, from Sandford), 115 (engraving, Inthronization of James II and Queen Mary, from Sandford), 122 (Coronation Lunch for George VI and Queen Elizabeth 1937, Frank Salisbury, Guildhall Art Gallery, Corporation of London). *Michael Holford*: pages 14 (Bayeux Tapestry, Musée de Bayeux), 23 (Bayeux Tapestry, Musée de Bayeux), 39 (Bayeux Tapestry, Musée de Bayeux). *Crown copyright*: pages 19 (engraving, 19th cent., Hampton Court Palace, Historic Royal Palaces), 21 (Woodmansterne Picture Library), 28 (Photo. A.C. Cooper), 30 (Photo. A.C. Cooper), 33 right (Kohinur diamond), 34 (Photo. A.C. Cooper), 36 (Photo. A.C. Cooper), 37 (Woodmansterne Picture Library), 40 centre and right (Photo. A.C. Cooper), 41 (Photo. A.C. Cooper), 43 (Photo. A.C. Cooper), 47, 50, 51 bottom (Photo. A.C. Cooper), 52 (Photo. A.C. Cooper), 53 left (Photo. A.C. Cooper), 53 right, 54 (Photo. A.C. Cooper), 94 (Woodmansterne Picture Library). *Mary Evans Picture Library*: pages 27 (print, 17th cent.), 51 top (woodcut, Jost Amman), 88 (miniature, the Coronation of Henry IV, Froissart). *Victoria and Albert Museum/V & A Picture Library*: pages 32–3 background (miniature, Babur in the Garden of Fidelity IM. 276–1913, Courtesy of the Trustees of the V&A), 45 (terracotta statuette of Mary II, *c.*1693, A.208 1946, Courtesy of the Trustees of the V&A). *British Museum*: page 42 (coin from the reign of Edward the Confessor), page 45 left (engraving, Coronation of William III and Mary II). *British Library*: page 46 right (miniature, COTT. CLAUD. B.4). *Lauros – Giraudon*: page 46 left (enamelled tomb plaque of Geoffrey of Anjou, 1150–60, Le Mans). *Woodmansterne Ltd*: pages 59, 72–3, 108 (coronation chair), 112, 127. *Westminster Abbey*: page 62 (miniature, coronation of a king and queen, Liber Regalis, courtesy of the Dean and Chapter of Westminster Abbey). *National Portrait Gallery, Publications Dept*: pages 64 (portrait of Elizabeth of York, Reg. No. 311), 67 (portrait of Elizabeth I, Reg. No. 5175), 98 (portrait of Mary I, by Master John 1544, Reg. No. 428). *Master and Fellows of Trinity College, Cambridge*: pages 76–7 (MS.O.3.59). *Ashmolean Museum, Oxford*: page 78 top (The Coronation of William and Mary, Sutherland Collection, Dept of Western Art). *The Hulton-Deutsch Collection*: pages 80, 90, 92, 106, 114, 118, 119, 120. *Illustrations taken from The Queen Elizabeth Coronation Souvenir 1953, printed by L.T.A. Robinson Ltd, London*: pages: 84, 86, 100, 101, 110, 116, 128. *Express Newspapers plc* (Illustrations taken from the Coronation Souvenir Book, 1937, a Daily Express Publication): pages 102, 104. *Front cover*: The Hulton-Deutsch Collection *Back cover*: left: Crown copyright right: Michael Holford *Line drawings* by Peter J. Taylor: pages 24–5, 79.

THE CORONATION CEREMONY AND THE CROWN JEWELS